Our True Identity and how our Feelings Create Life

Phillip

© Phillip 2022

All rights reserved. Except for the quotation of short passages for the purposes of criticism and review, no part of this publication may be reproduced, stored in a retrieval system, or transmitted in any form or by any means, electronic, mechanical, photocopying, recording, or otherwise, without the prior written permission of the Copyright Authority Ltd. or the publisher.

ISBN: 978-1-922784-11-7

First published in Australia August 2022

Layout and design by Clark & Mackay.

Printed by Clark and Mackay, Brisbane, Australia

TABLE OF CONTENTS

PREFACE v

INTRODUCTION 1

CHAPTER 1.
    Consciousness and the Quantum energy field. 15

CHAPTER 2.
    Self-realisation: Our true identity in the
    conscious quantum field 29
        All the power is within us. 57
        The Kingdom's power is within us - Jesus 61
        Paul's kingdoms power - christ within us 68
        Truth, trust, and faith - what is correct? 74
        The spiritual and human mind. 77

CHAPTER 3.
    Self-mastery: How to live divinely and manifest
    abundance in the quantum field. 85
        Quantum manifesting - the new way. 89
        How our feelings create our life 106

    Feelings and emotions - big difference. 110
    The Gospel of Thomas and feelings 120
    Your subconscious mind and feelings 126

CHAPTER 4.
    Stillness meditation: Why and how to connect to our higher eternal true self through a thoughtless state 139

CHAPTER 5.
    Conclusion. 149

APPENDIX 153

THANK YOU 155

PREFACE

This book is the merging of more than 5,000 non-fiction spiritual books that I have read over the past 40 years. I am sure you will find something new in this book and will become as excited as I was when I discovered this new quantum-aware world suddenly opened for me.

I trust that this book is for everyone who picks it up. This book will surely change anybody who is reading it. It is of as much significance to non-believers as to believers. There is specific unknown or mysterious knowledge that is now becoming more widely known and being confirmed by quantum science. It reveals that we are holy, sacred, and divine and that there is now also a new understanding of our reality and therefor a new and better way of living.

The information in this book is for anybody who wants to discover the truth of who they really, really are and who is looking for a technique, method, or strategy to live everyday life according to current scientific evidence. What is amazing about these revelations is that you only need to understand (comprehend) them once. After that you do not need any more knowledge, books or expertise but only need to experience and live your life accordingly.

Like driving a car, once you understand how to drive, you only need to practice improving. These truths will become integrated into your whole life. As you will see you will not need another teaching or teacher after this because your true self will lead you to all wisdom. This book is not at all about religion, although we do use some sacred scriptures. I explicitly also do not want to claim any originality.

You will not be able to read this book in one sitting as there really are too many exciting and challenging revelations condensed into a book of one hundred and fifty pages. It would be profitable to read this book more than once until you understand this technique or formula, after that you only need to follow your heart.

There are too many people to thank and acknowledge. I thank all the writers of all the books I have ever read, and if you have ever authored a book, I thank you too because maybe you influenced one of the writers of the books I have read.

INTRODUCTION

Please do not stop reading! As you will later see, there are no accidents in this universe. The divine journey that has delivered you this **message given in the form of <u>sayings</u> or <u>proverbs</u>** is no random event, and it did come your way for a reason. Every event in your life has happened for a reason and has also brought you to this moment in time to read the truths in this book which will forever set you free.

Do you know who you really are? There is nothing more important in this world and the greatest treasure to find is for you to wake up and discover the truth of who you really are and that the larger part of you is non-physical. We do give importance to so many things we do know do not matter. If you only collect stuff and do things and do not know who you really are, why you are here, and how to experience a happy life, life has no meaning, and you cannot experience true freedom and happiness.

You are not a victim of a cruel experiment, and you do not have to die before being able to realise what this universe and your life are all about. You need to stop being ignorant. If you do not know yourself, how can you be yourself? Our existence would feel more fulfilled and meaningful if we could find our deeper "beingness" and bring that into our life. The knowing of our own being and the connection to our higher self is the only answer to a fulfilled, joyful life. We are not our mind or body, but far superior to that.

Whether you are religious or not at all religious, this is for you. This is not an opinion, belief system, religion, or philosophy, but knowledge based on current scientific evidence. There will be no preaching but only a discussion of current scientific knowledge and what we know so far. In this age of information ignorance is really just a choice. Science is gathering knowledge faster than wisdom; therefore, we need to evaluate our wisdom regularly. The more science reveals, the more we discover our actual identity and true nature of who and what we really are. We also now discovered our true power in this reality.

Quantum science has done away with the old Newtonian fundamental principle of cause and effect (from your outer world), replacing it with a new quantum model where you are causing an effect by thinking and feeling (from your inner world) before an experience can occur, and it is beautiful. This new rediscovered knowledge shows that you create your own reality, so your life is supposed to feel good to you. It shows that you are totally free, that the way you think and feel creates your reality, so you need not be a victim of your circumstances any longer, and not be trapped in this material world. Suffering on this planet is only caused by you not knowing who you are.

You will realise that if you know who you really are, you can be, do and have whatever you want. **Your world is shaped by your knowledge of your true personal identity** and the thoughts that result from this understanding. To change your personal reality, you just need to change your thoughts about who you really are, your true identity. You are in control of your own destiny, and you need to walk the path yourself. To change your life, you cannot continue to think the same old thoughts and have the same old emotions as in the past. The problem is that your ego-mind (false sense of self) is just a by-product of evolution. Your ego-mind (false sense of self) is just a program in your subconscious mind and only contains old past thoughts. If you do not change your programmed thinking, you will always manifest the same old results as before.

It does not matter whether you are a Hindu, Jew, Christian, Muslim, Rasta Man, Buddhist or not religious at all. The evidence in front of you will convince you that there is a new understanding of the true nature of our own identity and reality and a new scientific technique or strategy for abundant living.

There really are only two core teachings that form the basis of all the knowledge that you will ever need to live a self-controlled free, peaceful, and fulfilled life. If you truly understand these two truths, you will actually understand everything. You will also understand your true identity of who you really are and also how you can create your future to forever live a happy and abundant life. You will discover that you are controlled by a mind-made program you wrongly believe is you. You will discover that you are already whole and who you always wanted and needed to be and that you can have whatever you always wanted to have. You will also realise that you need to create your own purpose (you're meaning for living) to make this world a better place for yourself and everybody else. No guru, pastor, priest, ritual, etc, except yourself is needed to help you to discover and experience your eternal true self and how to live life effortlessly and in abundance. It is so simple, but you may not see it.

Understanding is far better than just acquired knowledge. The universe always invites you to question everything and assists you in coming to your own intelligent conclusions. Solomon, one of the wisest people ever said, "Wisdom is the principal thing; therefore, get wisdom; and with all thy getting get understanding.

By understanding this knowledge, you will also realise you have to be and can only be your own guide and teacher. Trust and rely only on yourself. Listen to the intuition of your inner being who has got all the answers you need.

You can really now rediscover your eternal true self and be the most remarkable, accurate expression of yourself as a human being and realise you are magnificent, perfect, and whole. <u>Jesus even said, "if you do not know yourself, you will live in vain, and you will be vanity (useless, empty)."</u> If you compare this knowledge from Jesus with the sayings of Buddha, Lao Tzu, and other mystics, they basically all followed the same core principles, and they lived 500 years before Jesus was born. If you are spiritual and Jesus is important to you, the sayings and universal truths in this book were also his two fundamental teachings. Jesus did not plagiarise these truths, they are simply eternal truths that we do now understand a lot better, thanks to science.

If you take the time to understand and use this mystery or secret knowledge, it will equally always work for you. Krishna Murti said, "The most awkward thing to learn is something we think we already know." Sometimes you need to look at life from a different perspective, and when the real is seen, the false falls away by itself. These are not only just eternal universal truths but also the basis of all Jesus's teachings. Jesus' two doctrines and their core ideas are the same as most other spiritual teachings through the ages and are of the greatest teachings ever. They form the basis for successful living and as being mentioned, have now been confirmed by current scientific evidence.

Mystics, Sages, Jesus, and others spoke about a universal creative power 2000 years ago that was available to everyone, and it was this creative power that fascinated everybody around them. This creative power and its simplicity which makes it hard to understand, is available all the time and is available to be used by every one of us in the universe. We are never alone; this infinite power has always been within and around us. Jesus said that because of this creative power, we can experience joy and happiness here and now and we only need to follow our higher inner self for optimum guidance.

Jesus said that the more you understand (comprehend) this knowledge, the more you will be given what you desire. Jesus's whole life was based on successful living. These teachings were also the basis of all his other teachings. He even asked his followers, "Don't you understand this story, then how will you understand (comprehend) any stories of this kind?" explaining that if you do not understand this knowledge of his, how will you understand all other truths. He also explains that to the degree you understand this knowledge, to that degree this creative power will work and be effective for you.

His teachings were an affirmation of the availability of this universal power and a revelation of who we really are.

You are not a victim or a poor little me with an earth suit, you are an infinite, immortal, and eternal energy being. You just need to put a little bit of work in and grasp these two truths, and your life will be from now on and will remain to be forever free and happy. Through gaining this knowledge we now have a method and can live a self-empowered happy and joyous life. It is also very understandable and easy to remember. You just need to know how to do it. I do think that the way Jesus explains these universal truths is not the only example, but it is the best example of who we really are and of how to use this creative power to get the most out of it.

If you fully understand these teachings or truths, you will understand everything and you will open the store of this way of abundant living for yourself. There is something better on the other side of this. There is enough for everybody to always live in abundance and luxury, but you will only attract what you truly feel worthy of and honestly expect. You will realise that life is also not a competition at all, just a play. This infinite creative power has no beginning and no end and therefore can be experienced right now and into eternity.

Again, I want to acknowledge that this is not a belief system, a religion, an opinion, or a philosophy. ***This is knowledge and a technique that you just need to fully understand.*** Your higher true self in you already knows everything. So, please ***do not believe anything*** that is not in your experience, but only that which you understand and resonates in your heart. You also need to test and try and see yourself whether this is effective and is the truth.

We also must choose to find our own meaning and purpose in life from this revived and new knowledge. In the New Testament the word repents just means that you need to change your way of thinking. You need to repent (change your way of thinking) and realise who you really are as a self-aware being and discover this creative power within and around you and learn how to use it effectively for abundant living. The purpose of this creative energy power within and among us is to use it as a powerful tool to operate in this world. The best technology for us to operate in this world is therefore inside our own bodies.

This creative power and the technique to use it are forever available to everyone in the universe. Life is on our side and working in our best interest. Jesus proclaimed that the knowledge of this creative energy power is his good news and that this is the way to do things and open the unlimited abundant stores of the universe forever for all of us. You also do not need to go anywhere but draw all your experiences like a magnet towards you. We can now be, have and achieve all we ever desire.

Quantum physics is telling us that everything we thought was physical is not physical at all but is just energy vibrating at different frequencies. Energy is all that there is, there is nothing else and it is always in motion. Energy can be explained as a force that has the capability to do work and the influence to cause an action. Everything is energy and energy can never be destroyed, meaning nothing ever disappears. The energy form can only change form. This then also means that all our desires already exist in the universe.

Deep within us we all are just part of a one giant limitless energy field that vibrates at different frequencies. This quantum energy field is a unified field of pure potentiality, intelligence, beingness, self-awareness and consciousness. Everything including us is one with this unseen unified energy field. All the seen (visible) was born out of this unseen (invisible) field. This field has been described as a powerful creative energy force within and among us.

Words cannot really describe this **powerful creative energy field,** but we use the following different descriptions:
1. Mystics and philosophers like to describe it as awareness or consciousness. (The names Krishna, Shiva, Christ, and Buddha all refer to this infinite power which we understand as consciousness.)
2. Science prefers to call this the quantum energy field, the unified field, the divine matrix, or consciousness etc.
3. Paul used the words "Christ in you," or "the anointing," or "the Spirit of the Lord," or "the Kingdom of God."

4. The church today also uses words like "the anointing" or "Christ in you", or "the Holy Spirit in you", or "God in you."
5. Jesus called this powerful energy field "The Kingdom of God," or "the Spirit of the Lord" or "the anointing."
6. The secular world has many names which try to explain and describe this energy field of power, and the main ones include the following:

Quantum energy field	Universe
Consciousness Awareness	God field
Divine matrix	Divinity or Divine Spirit
Source energy	Source of creation
Universal mind	Essence of the universe
Kingdom of God	I am or Beingness
Brahman	Oneness etc.

The **properties of this quantum energy field** (or essence of the universe) which is just infinite eternal energy **in consciousness,** can be described as follows:
− *It is a fluid-like substance of energy that ripples in waves.*
− It is unseen. (There is no day or night here, no colour, and no place where it is not.)
− It is all-pervading and everywhere. (It is oneness.)
− It is eternal. (It is timeless.)
− It is not perceivable. (It is undefinable.)
− It is beyond distance. (Distance does not exist.)
− It is not an object. (It is formless.)
− It cannot be measured. (It is spaceless.)
− It is not even oneness. (It is nothingness.)
− There are no persons here, no you or me.
− You cannot disconnect yourself from it.
− You cannot reach it through your imagination.
− It remains unaffected by anything, no one possesses it.
− It does not come and go, and it is not cold or hot here.
− Nothing needs to be done or undone, become, be changed or be fixed here.
− There is not an above or below here.
− There is nothing behind or in front of it.

- It cannot leave because it never came.
- The essence of who we are is here.
- There is no history, relationships or story here.
- You cannot be you here, but it is here in you.
- There is no heaven or hell, male or female here.
- You can't find or lose it by being super good or super bad.
- It is not a physical place, but this is where you, Jesus, Buddha, and all beings come from and return.
- All the planets exist because of this field of energy waves.
- Your body and mind are its house or temple on earth.
- This energy essence is everything including Jesus and us.

There are no thoughts or emotions here but every one of us speaks to this quantum energy field continuously throughout the day with our thoughts and emotions, and the universe reacts continuously by creating accordingly.

Scientists are telling us now that all possibilities and all that we desire already exist in this energy field via quantum energy. *In this energy field of possibilities, we are already whole and healed, joy, happiness and peace are everywhere, and all our desires are met.*

We all are participating in the way this reality unfolds and evolve. There are actually only two components necessary to participate in and live life the way you were intended to live it, and they are,
1. Self-realisation (who am I really as an energy being).
2. Self-mastery (how to live life as an energy being).

These principal routes to freedom and happiness were also the basis of all Jesus' teachings and his two main doctrines (ideologies, dogmas) that he was teaching.

You will also discover that you are an immortal, infinite being just having a temporal (finite) transient earthly experience. Everything you need for well-being and freedom can be reached right here and now on earth. Jesus, one of the greatest teachers ever said in Psalm 82:6 that we are all gods and indeed children of the Most High. He suggests here that we are all already whole, powerful, divine and in control of this universal energy field's power. Jesus even cursed a fig tree to demonstrate this power and the fig tree withered by the next day. Later, he also said that we would do more extraordinary things than him by commanding a mountain to move, and it would.

You will only attract and manifest your desires in alignment with who you really think you are, your realised personality or state of being and to what degree you understand this knowledge of this energy power. Your life will improve when you change and improve the way you think about yourself and this energy field. You need to change your way of thinking about this universal energy within you and its way of doing things. You also need to realise who you really are in this energy field. This creative energy power is available where you are and reacts according to your understanding of this hidden truth.

All I want to do is to convince you not to doubt who you already are, your true identity and genuine personality, because according to that is what you will attract into your life. You will not attract what you want but what and who you think you really are. ***Success is a side effect of who you are.*** At the core of the universe and us, there is only this vibrational energy power and the seen is just an illusion of the oscillations of this energy field interacting with the forces in the energy field. What we call mind and matter are one and the same substance (energy) except the only difference is in the degree (frequency) of vibration.

You can change this energy electrically and magnetically with your thinking which changes the energy field inside and around you, creating (manifesting) new experiences.

Seeing that the seen is from this limitless unseen energy field there is also no lack or shortage in this universe so everybody on earth can now manifest anything according to their desires. Everything already exists so there is no such thing as creating as we only create by manifesting.

If you do start to adapt this factual knowledge, your life will be a lot better, bigger, and happier than ever before. You can control and decide to which thoughts you attach your emotions to, to create your own joyful life. When you put this new knowledge into action, you will realise something will always happen to you according to your true feelings. If you can feel it in your heart, it will happen. So your mind will always need to follow the true feelings of your heart.

Using sayings or proverbs, I can only point you towards these truths. I myself have got a burning desire to know what truth is above all else and am doing my best to live what I have learned and am still learning. I am not saying follow or believe me. I am saying, do not trust anybody, including me, just listen to your own heart who has got all the truth and then test these facts. All truth is perfect and complete and already inside you. You will resonate with this message if you are ready to receive it. You will also realise that if you want any information about how to live life, you will have to go within to your higher eternal true self as thousands of mystics do for guidance, and not to any outside source as you used to do previously.

The fact that all these eternal truths are now substantiated by current scientific evidence will also help you completely trust, understand, and use them confidently. It will help you fully trust the truth of who you really are and the availability of this power within that you never really knew existed before. This is not information for which you need belief, blind faith, or any other sources. You just need to **realise and understand these truths**.

My only goal for you is to think about what the universal energy field is thinking and for you to know and understand the workings of this powerful energy field that not many people know exist. You also need to question yourself and see whether you genuinely know yourself, your true identity and your real personality. Ramana Maharshi said, "Until you know who you are, all your knowledge is only learned ignorance." Before you can know anything else, you need to know that you are a self-aware superhuman being. **Whom you think you are and who you really are can be quite different, and this needs to be explored.** If you discover your true original nature, your restlessness will go away.

Everything seen including you is just energy appearing, so you only appear on this planet as a mind and body in an earth suit. If you think you are just a material being with a mind and body then you will always live the life of a material-being instead of as a spiritual, limitless, timeless, eternal energy being. The actual aware you, are an eternal, limitless energy identity deep inside your mind and body, and you do need to separate the two identities for effective living. You are already forever and endless.

You only suffer on this planet because you are, or you became unaware of your true unchanged nature. Although your personality is the result of all your past thoughts, emotions, and actions, you will discover that you can change your personality to the real you by changing your thinking. Your personal reality will then change effortlessly to whatever you desire in your future. You have the ability in you to be able to change your thoughts and to be in control of your own destiny. You really need to change your limiting beliefs. So, you do need to rediscover, recognise, and accept who you really, really are otherwise you will miss the best part of being human and enjoy life.

I honestly believe that it will be a great tragedy if you miss this amazing simple truth *that the source of all creation is not on your outside (externally) but within you (internally), and also miss the knowledge of what the true nature of the source of creation, this reality really is.* This new way of operating in this world where there is enough for everybody is so that everybody can live happy and in luxurious abundance. You will also learn the importance of the fact that the universe only gives you what you think you are worthy of and expect to receive. That is why it is so crucial that you need to know and see clearly who you indeed are.

I am not telling you something you do not already know deep inside yourself. You are the knower of all things, and you just need to read, understand, and get this. Only the knowledge of these truths will give you absolute peace and happiness. *Your mind always needs proof before it will believe and trust anything. Truth cannot be created but it can only be discovered.* The knowledge of these truths is now available and can be discovered. The door is open, so why do you want to stay in prison? These revelations will not come easily, but it will be worth it. Do you want to discover and fulfil your reason for being? Do you have the courage to see these truths?

You are who you are, even if you think different. When you see your true identity clear, you will feel whole, complete, free, and happy. It has been said, ***"The one who has found himself, found everything." Know who you are!***

Acceptance happens when reality is seen clearly. As I have experienced, you will then also discover inner peace and freedom as never before.

As you heal yourselves, you will heal others, and will feel as if you do not need as much as before for fulfilment. You are always supposed to take care of yourself first, perhaps there may be something you are missing.

Remember this is not an easy-read storybook by any means. Discovering who you are takes energy. Although these are simple truths, you need to focus and put the time into understanding this and to figure it all out. ***It can initially be difficult to really comprehend all these sayings and powerful pointers to the truth.*** Do not read it just with your mind but also with your inner awareness. Sages do take about twelve years full-time to learn all these truths from a guru. I also do know I am being repetitive at times, but it is very necessary to comprehend all this knowledge.

You do not only can now predict your future, but you can create it. Do not stop reading until you understand the chapter on how to manifest abundance which will bring all the information together. Only then all this information will make sense and will it become your reality forever. You also need to try and put all this knowledge to the test and experience to see whether it is reliable.

You only live once, but fortunately that is forever, do not give up on yourself. This book came to you for a reason.

We need to throw away our old knowledge and start to discover these new truths that are now available. The truths that you are going to discover here will not make you a religious person, it will give you peace, happiness, and abundance and will set you free forever and ever.

The purpose of life is to find happiness, which is also the knowing of our own true eternal self. Knowing means to know and be that. **We all are whole, holy, kind, and divine and just do not realise it. To know our true identity and know that we are not just human beings, is genuinely the solution for all our suffering and all the suffering on earth. Listen and look beyond these sayings with an open heart.** Do not run away from your true endless freedom. **Once you can really see, you will never again be able to unsee.**

Also, remember to not look for the true self, the looking creates separation and distance, just be the true self.

IN A NUTSHELL

What would your answer be if somebody asks you to tell them something about yourself, who are you? Who do you take yourself to be? Most of us have a false idea of ourselves and are under the **delusion that our body and mind are who we indeed are.** We do now know that this is a **delusion** and not the truth.

We do need to find who dwells in our own self. We do now know that there is **a place deep inside us** where we are never changing and have an **unchanging, eternal nature which is our real true nature.** Our true nature is changeless, untouchable, the imperishable eternal self. This is where we are perfect in harmony.

In the vast ocean of awareness/consciousness, our unchanging eternal part is just an empty space, a no thing, a nothingness posing as everything. Our true nature is not an object (entity) but is like an empty space moving through space, an uncreated timeless awareness of our unconscious mind. In this vast ocean of conscious awareness, all things happen in our presence. This is where we as the pure awareness experience imperfection, where we as the timeless experience time and as the spaceless experiencing space. This is where we are conscious of our unconsciousness. This is where we as consciousness are dancing inside our infinite stillness. *In this realm, even I, the most profound concept is just perceived or imagined.*

The instant you can see the truth that you are the unchanging one in an ocean of awareness and the unchanging and you are one,

and you genuinely have true freedom. When we recognise our ***true eternal unchanging nature***, the ***delusion*** of whom we thought we were is broken, and we will indeed be free.

When we become conscious, we start witnessing our own thoughts. Our thoughts arise like clouds in the state of consciousness. Your mind gets to be controlled by your consciousness/awareness and not controlled or managed by your ego (false sense of self) mind. ***Our suffering will then also come to an end and there will be a new confidence without fear because every thought can come to us, but no thought will or can be stuck on us.***

Once you can see this unchanging eternal nature of yourself, you will really know ***your true self*** and never be able to unsee this truth again.

You will realise that you are a creator and that there are no limits to what you can create or manifest for yourself in this life. Your unchanging nature then is just you without you, so just be you without you!

Do not prevent yourself from experiencing life, let everything come, it is just a song or dance of the universe. Even your false ego-self (mind and body) is born out of consciousness, so enjoy that also. This is a mortal body, but the immortal is using it. You can now enjoy the natural realm without being attached to it. Your natural world will pass but where it comes from will never pass.

You are the seed of the world that is waking up from this hypnotic state, do not sleep now.

CHAPTER 1

CONSCIOUSNESS AND THE QUANTUM ENERGY FIELD

It has now been generally accepted that beyond all created things lies the womb of creation namely pure consciousness as a pure completeness that does not begin anywhere and is therefore beginningless. Because reality exists, there must be a fundamental component that exists by itself. Pure consciousness has now been accepted by many as the fundamental component of reality out of which everything is made, containing nothing but only the potential of energy and thus everything. ***This means everything evolves out of consciousness,*** and everything then is consciousness. ***Consciousness is really all there is.***

Pure consciousness then is the perfect natural state and life before it comes into manifestation where there are no objects (nothing, nobody), no thoughts (mind) and is spaceless and timeless. Pure consciousness is known by itself. In consciousness all possibilities and infinite realities exist. As it is before the subject/object split, pure consciousness is **complete and whole in itself** and therefore goes beyond today's physics. We will most probably never be able to explain it entirely, but that consciousness exists is indisputable.

Consciousness, defined by the Oxford dictionary is the state of being aware of and responsive to one's surroundings. Consciousness cannot see or experience itself, so it needs to manifest to see and experience itself. **The universe and creation are the contents and an activity, an action, a play of this consciousness experiencing itself, using a quantum energy field.** Everything you see is consciousness. The mind, the body and the world located inside consciousness are only made from consciousness and are not a container of any memory. Consciousness is who we are. Consciousness controls reality and we really do not know and will never know where consciousness comes from because it is not contained and cannot be measured.

The universe in consciousness is beautiful, complete, peaceful, and perfect and is just energy in motion (just a dance of energy). Everything is an expression of consciousness that is self-aware **and there is only one consciousness which also then means that it includes you.**

The ultimate purpose of infinite consciousness is to express its free will through a finite consciousness. For the infinite consciousness to have a localised experience of itself, it needs to create a finite world, and needs to project the illusion of being a finite identity with a mind and body. Consciousness is experiencing and informing itself through its creations that involve us. **Consciousness can be aware of itself through us as creations.** We all are just simply different expressions of this one quantum energy field that is immersed in consciousness. The mind is the play of consciousness once it starts to make things. We as consciousness are aware of and the witness of all appearances and phenomena including time and space.

So, it is consciousness and the act of us participating in it that creates the stuff the universe is made of. John Wheeler said, "We live in a participating universe that continuously builds itself." The universe is continuously being built (it is expanding) by us and added to itself through consciousness. The body enables consciousness to taste experiences. **The universe then cannot exist without us.** As a person we are inside this body, but as consciousness this body is inside us. The whole existing universe immersed in consciousness consists of just energy that is never created and cannot ever be destroyed. This is the energy that connects all. All this energy is interdependent and interconnected as one with no separation, and we are just an individual vibrational frequency of it. Everything you look at around you are just one quantum energy field vibrating in frequencies from an all-connecting field proven at Cern in Switzerland in 2012. **There is no empty space in the universe. Empty space is also filled with quantum energy that you just cannot see.** This energy or essence permeates everything in the universe and essentially is unified as one.

This godly unseen quantum energy field we are one with consists of quantum energy waves which itself is part of this conscious field with no mind that reacts on its own. In this timeless and spaceless dimension, there is no past and there is no future, no form, no thing, and no image. It is this non-identity posing as everything. This whole universe including our old idea of "God" is entirely made up of this energy that science calls a quantum energy field. This divine unseen quantum energy field has always been, is everything and is everywhere.

What we have discovered so far is that this quantum energy field is a fluid-like substance of energy that ripples in strange waves. So, if you go **deep inside** yourself, a fluid-like substance of energy that ripples in strange waves exist. There is no time, no space, no sound, no you, no creation, no creator but only this godly energy field that is the container of everything. If we **go back far** enough before time, there was a point where only this quantum energy field existed, which only had the possibility to form **quantum waves and quantum particles** (protons, matter). Although there was only energy, all the energy was interconnected, and everything was ordered and perfect.

Since time and space began everything changed and according to Deepak Chopra mind and matter first emerge exactly alike as invisible ripples in the quantum field which form pattens as they run into ripples from the following fields, **up-quark field, down-quark field, electron field and the Higgs field**. Interference patterns, which are like rippled imprints of waves left on a sandy beach get set up, and only then do recognizable objects such as quarks and electrons forming proton particles begin to appear, and the universe now consists of quantum waves (unseen energy) and quantum particles (matter, seen energy). The Higgs field proven by science is what gives the proton particles their mass was, discovered in 2012 in the Cern Hadron Collider, a particle accelerator in Switzerland.

The ripples of the fluid-like quantum energy in the quantum field are now becoming waves of energy vibrating at a frequency on what we call a Planck scale. They are called Planck **oscillators** and are full of information in the form of energy. Every energy frequency carries different information. These oscillators, which are oscillating (vibrating at a frequency) interact with each other as well as with four forces. Only two are of importance namely **gravity** and the **electromagnetic force**. The other two are the **strong nuclear force and a weak nuclear force.** Know that there are no other forces known to man that can play a role in our everyday life. Out of these energy forces and fields of waves, we get the formation of subatomic quantum particles (**quarks**) responsible for forming of all **proton** particles and then **atoms** and **matter.** These subatomic quantum particles (matter) are the smallest building blocks known in the universe. They are called up-quark particles, down-quark particles and electron particles and not important neutrinos. These quarks are found inside proton particles and neutron particles, which together with electrons form atoms. There are about 10^{80} proton particles in the universe (Eddington number). They are then just waves of bundles of energy influenced mainly by the electromagnetic force and the gravitational force.

This then also means that all matter (physical mass) does not exist the way we used to think it did. It really just exists as bundles of energy-containing information.

These quantum proton particles are full of information in the form of energy vibrating at specific frequencies. The seen universe (matter) is made up of atoms consisting of these particles. A shell is a shell because it is the frequency within at which the energy is vibrating.

The total energy of our whole universe is zero. There is positive energy e.g., mass, radiation, and there is negative energy in gravity, and together they add up to zero. So, our universe appearing out of nothing violates no laws.

We are beings made from clusters of atoms (local energy fields) that are connected and interact with each other. Every person has about 75 trillion cells, and each cell has about 75 trillion atoms, and as mentioned before, each atom consists of protons (consisting of quarks), neutrons (consisting of quarks), and electrons. What is so beautiful is that billions of cells divide, and billions of chemical changes happen each second in our bodies. The same thing happens all around us and alsoeverywhere in nature.

It took nature millions of years to get us to this place where we are now, and this makes us so much more special. Therefore reality (the quantum energy field) is deep inside and around us where time and place do not exist. It only consists of an energy field with energy vibrating in waves (different frequencies).

This then is just a vibrational universe. There is only this one timeless unending powerful energy field (unseen energy) manifesting different objects (seen matter, particles). Einstein said that objects (particles, matter, humans, etc.) are not in space but are extensions of space.

When time came out of the timeless, physical particles (matter), initially only hydrogen atoms and helium atoms formed, forming stars and then new atoms, then some stars began to explode and separate but *energetically the particles (matter) remained interconnected through what is known as quantum entanglement* which has recently been discovered by science.

A HOLOGRAPHIC UNIVERSE:
Inside each of the proton particles in you and inside the rest of the 10^{80} proton particles that exist in the universe is exactly the same universal information *holographically, meaning this is a holographic universe (never-ending pattern).* In an authentic *hologram* every piece of the *hologram is a carbon copy* of the original and it has all the information about the whole of and every other piece in the structure. There is nothing in this energy field that is not also perfectly mirrored

inside you. We are all just small holograms (pieces) from a giant hologram (universe). This means that this one holographic universe is just a reflection of us, and we are just a reflection of it. ***If you are a hologram, that then also means that you are not powerless at all as we thought in the past, you have the same power as this giant hologram.*** All the available information of the world then exists inside every single proton particle in existence, including every proton in every cell of your body. Every proton in each cell of your body is all then just a hologram of the universe.

Each proton particle is also constantly and instantaneously getting updated (they interact with each other) with any added new information across any distance due to quantum entanglement. Entanglement proved beyond a doubt in 1997 means once something is joined, and once something begins as a whole, even though it is separated physically by distance or light-years, ***energetically everything is still interconnected***.

Although they are a distance apart, all the available information in one proton particle is interconnected (entangled) to all the information of nearly all the other protons in the universe. We live in a connected world. The same information that is holographically present in every proton always stays the same because of entanglement (interconnection) through what scientists speculate and are calling "wormholes." This also means that every one of the 10^{80} quantum proton particles in us and the universe is forever continuously getting updated with current new information from each other as the universe expands.

This also means then that it is not just our brain that transmits and receives thoughts. Every cell in our body has memory and the ability to transmit and receive thoughts. Our mind then includes our body and our brain. Our brain is really just an antenna, a frequency analyser and the frequency get displayed in it is the mind.

Everything in existence including us proven by science, is just one vibrational reality of energy that is vibrating at different frequencies. So, everything we see in this universe is us and is just us manifesting from this unseen vibration of energy vibrating at different levels of frequencies. A frequency is the vibrational level and is measured in cycles per second. You really are just a vibrational energy being. Even what you smell, taste, etc. are also just translations of vibrational energy frequencies.

Thoughts, emotions, and feelings are also all just energy. When you are having a thought and emotion, you are creating an energy vibrational frequency, and when you change your thought and emotion, you change the level of the vibrational frequency.

Again, we do now know that in this quantum energy field, all the proton particles (vibrational matter) appear to be interconnected and **communicate with each other**. This cause the universe to evolve by feeding and updating itself continuously with new information as it changes through entanglement where everything is joined as one. This is also the reason why **we only need to look within for all our knowledge and guidance where all the current information of the universe is always available and getting updated continuously through entanglement**. This is also how the universe grows, evolves, expands, and becomes wise and more conscious of itself.

There is nothing outside the universe, there is only one existence. Buddha, Jesus, Holy Spirit, and us, are all part of this one existence, this powerful quantum energy field.

For the energy field to know and experience itself, it radiates itself into this universe through everyone and everything. This divine energy field is creating everything from itself and manifests itself in this creation through vibrational frequency energy impulses to whatever it desires (the creator and creation then are the same source).

So, you can understand that these energy particles including us are not real but potentially can be anything. We are just a highly organised local energy field of this universal energy feeding information back to itself.

*We really are just stardust with inner self-awareness wrapped in skin. We are all made of stardust (physical matter) which as explained then means that all the current information of the universe is also independently in every **proton particle inside each of the 75 trillion*** *cells in our human body. This energy field is in us, and we are in it. We as this quantum field are really just expanding to know and to experience itself through the seen and unseen universe.*

All the current information of the world is in its totality and separately collected in each proton particle in all the 75 trillion atoms inside every 75 trillion cells inside us and every proton updates continuously as the world is changing. Everything then that ever happened on this planet is still remembered by every proton particle in our body, because our body is just a piece of this holographic planet. Therefore, we can and need to go to our inner higher self to get all current information. This information in each proton is always current and available to us now from a timeless vibrating energy field within. We experience these vibrating energy waves with our awareness and feelings and also have the ability to interact with this energy field. We do know that our genes essentially also consist of current information.

The ultimate truth is that oneness of this energy field is and will forever be the only reality being governed by consciousness. So "God," us, and the material world are just one quantum energy field consisting of energy that can be visible (seen matter) and energy that is invisible (unseen energy) which can do whatever it desires to do.

The universe is just this quantum energy field, divinity, oneness playing with itself, and we are the universe.

Humans are an image or manifestation in the flesh of this non-physical unseen quantum energy field (universe). The universe is within our body. We are that within which the universe moves. We are the universe pretending we are not. The universe (the quantum energy field) which is us, is experiencing itself as a human being. *We as humans are something the universe (energy field) is doing.*

All life, space and time is just a magnificent appearance and just a play, an activity of this godly divine energy field in consciousness. There is no place where this one energy field is not, so it is in "God," you and me, and everything we see. There is really only one "I am" and we are all it. We are everything and everything is us. We are all then one and in harmony and unity with everybody and everything that exists and there is nothing outside us, this creative energy field. There is then also no you or anybody else outside of this energy field.

We are not from somewhere else but are all interconnected and part of this one energy world. According to our current acceptable scientific knowledge (what we know so far) creation energy in itself is enough to create itself. That which creates all, manifests all. Creation itself is creating itself. Existence is there without being created and it comes out of nothing. There are no other forces in this energy field that can be discovered to say differently. As mentioned before, we have given this field many names e.g., the universe, "God," but it has all the same essence, namely energy.

You can say that everything we see in this godly energy field is "God', you, and everybody else in disguise. We are not separate but are an expression of this energy field. (We are the creator and the creation we are living in.) We are the source of all things in the world. Ultimately reality cannot be explained due to the lack of linguistic words, and we genuinely just do not know. We can never truly know it and make full knowledge out of it This energy field cannot be fully understood and is really unknowable, but we can experience it by melting into it.

We are just a manifestation of this energy field pretending that we are not. This energy field manifests and sees itself through its instrument, our minds. This energy field sees into this world through our eyes. Whatever the universe desires, it manifests, so there is no lack or shortage of anything in this material universe because everything manifests out of this energy that is unlimited in supply. The quantum energy field then needs and desires nothing from anyone and that includes our idea of praise, worship, and offerings towards it.

We were this timeless and limitless energy field that are in consciousness before we came here. God is just a religious name, and mystics often use the word I or I am for this energy field. All existence (reality), including "God" exists then in energy form where there is no separation and of which we are all inseparably a part of and are one with. At the core of everything there is virtually no reality and no solid matter (particles) but there is only quality (only a single energy field that ripples in strange waves).

The energy field does not exclude anything from itself. It is everything including happiness, love, good, evil, emotional pain, order, chaos etc, etc. We really need to understand that **all human qualities exist in this energy field** because this energy field is all characters simultaneously.

These human qualities are all appearances and are all just mental, intellectual concepts because we do not know who we really are and are divided from our true identity. All is well in the perfection of all that is and there are no exceptions. Evil (darkness) is not the opposite but just the lack of good (light) and not a thing to compete against but to be accepted as aspects of the same energy in our reality. Know also that the universe will never but never test you. Emotional pain is just an invitation to burn the ego objective mind, the false sense of self.

It is these appearances that cause suffering, but in reality, we do not really suffer ourselves because we are the observers of all this. We do not need any help, motivation, or psychotherapy for our past emotions, we are whole, perfect, and complete and just need to realise this and be our true eternal identity, and the negative human qualities will disappear effortlessly. We just need to constantly surrender our minds to our true higher inner selves We also need to know that our thoughts and choices have something to do with our destiny. We are vibrationally living in a vibrational universe that reacts only to our thoughts, emotions, and feelings and not to our senses. This quantum energy field reacts to our thoughts, emotions, and feelings, and we co-create our reality accordingly. This universe is just a vibration of energy, and our thoughts, emotions and feelings are just vibrations of energy, and if you generate a powerful thought and emotion, it will manifest in your life as an experience.

We will discover that we all are one with this energy field, and there is nothing else in existence. At the core level of us, there is no us but just this **divine energy field** that is timeless, formless, everywhere and in everything, there is no separation or demarcation. This is the abiding formless presence that is the source and infinite eternal substance of all that exists.

It does not matter what we call this energy source, as long as we realise that we all originated from this same energy source of all life.

We must be similar to what we came from, and because we are not separate from it at all, our higher self is perfect, almighty, all-knowing, and divine already.

It would be regrettable sad if we believe that we are nothing else but just a mind (the activity of thought) and a body. The truth is that we are not our minds or our body. There is no real me, only energy that is transformed and appears as me. We are just spirit energy that is vibrating beyond our seen body. We need to understand that energy and vibration are more fundamental than matter.

We are all immortal non-physical energy. We do not really exist; we were never born and can never die. We are energy just having a human experience. We are all infinite beings that originated not from our parents but from this source of all existence. This energy field is where Jesus, Buddha, and every one of us returns to as energy and awareness at the end of our earthly experience. The bible says that "God's" spirit, power, or energy is in us but in the end, it is just one essence or substance namely energy.

Creation again, is just consciousness experiencing itself. When we say I am, we refer to ourselves as consciousness and not us as a person. We are infinite consciousness and made ourselves as an object to experience ourselves. Everything in our physical reality is all finite or temporary coming out of an infinite consciousness. The physical object (us) and the true eternal self are connected and have a relationship to its source in infinite consciousness since forever. The problem is that since we can think, we believe we are only physical objects, which we are not but we really are just energy in an empty space.

We are the beautiful beings that the universe, "God" quantum energy field decided to manifest here on earth, at this time in eternity. Reality then is the activity of "God's" mind. This energy field, "God" became you so that you can become this energy field here on earth. The real you then are this energy field, "God" who can never die. We need to learn to be this non-physical energy field, "God" and not just the physical object in the field.

To wake up to the truth of who we are must be our main aim in life, and this is the most essential knowledge for a human to obtain to live the ultimate fulfilled life. If we do not know ourselves, whatever we do will still be just the activity of deception. Eckard Tolle said, "Even if you have great material wealth, but you do not know yourself, you are still a beggar, you are still a slave to your mind."

We need to improve our knowing. We need to change and expand the view we have of ourselves, our self-image and then everything will change. To find our purpose in life will be impossible without finding ourselves first, and if we know and be ourselves, our purpose and everything else will follow at the same time. If we can manifest from the wholeness of who we really are, we will always produce the best results and be able to transform ourselves into a new person instead of only improving ourselves. There is pure goodness, kindness, and greatness in every person on earth and **we really are so much more than we are letting ourselves be.**

We all at times pretend we know and understand things that we really do not know or **understand** at all. This can prevent us from developing to our full potential and enjoying life to its fullest. To believe in or to have blind faith in, instead of trust, is to accept what you are told without you understanding or questioning it, but with this knowledge here, **no faith or belief is necessary.** You only need to get and understand this to accomplish anything you desire. We cannot from a human perspective comprehend who we really are. However, I really do think that quantum physics helped us a lot to understand the true nature of our own reality, ourselves, and our true universal identity.

As we will see where quantum physics has not yet fully explained to us who we are and how to operate in this universe, the spiritual world is making it much clearer to us. I do believe that Jesus, Buddha, and most other mystics completely understood their true identity as a union with "God "and also realised this creative power from within them. We are part of and not separate from the experiences in our life. Please take time and do not stop before you are sure you do know, are convinced, and understand these life-changing revelations of who you already are and this method to create your life appropriately that is now much clearer than ever before.

This knowledge does not need to be spiritual but only be logical. This is the way logically and there is no other way. Are you willing to see and understand your true nature?

CHAPTER 2

SELF-REALISATION: OUR TRUE IDENTITY IN THE CONSCIOUS QUANTUM ENERGY FIELD

Are you consciously aware of who you really are? You will find supreme happiness when you find your true self. To live a fulfilled life, it is of the utmost importance to understand our true identity and our personality of who we really are. Your identity is not found in the physical world. The physical part of us is just a temporary formation in the field of consciousness. The non-physical part of us is who we really are and who we were before we came into this body, and this larger part of us still exist. We are dimensional beings living a dimensional life and can never cease to exist. There is no separation between what is physical and what is non-physical. **The authentic self is a field of all possibilities in consciousness awareness** which is using a vibrating energy field to experience itself.

Everything already exists in this field, so **as conscious awareness we can choose which physical reality we want to experience.** As conscious awareness we chose to manifest a body and mind to experience life in this virtual physical reality. Our bodies now have been created in our minds as constructs from perceptions and sensations coming from translating vibrations to create a virtual reality, but we are not whom we see in the mirror. Our virtual reality, which is all just an appearance did cause and help us to forget who we really are. So, if we then want to be the real us, we will need to get rid of what is just a limited story, an appearance and unreal. **We will also need to change the concept of ourselves as not only being the body and mind (a physical part), but as awareness (a non-physical part) itself.**

Science has now proven to us again who we actually are in this physical reality. This is a vibrational universe, and we are all an evolving complex pattern of energy vibrating in it. Who we are is the same as what we came from. We were always energy and will always only be just energy. Each one of us consists of an electromagnetic energy field stretching up to 3 meters around us. **We really are boundless and infinite vibrational quantum energy beings vibrating at specific frequencies. Each one of us is a magnetic vibrational pattern of this energy field, a fractal or individualisation. Each one of us is a unique expression or appearance of this infinite energy field.**

We are this boundless energy that appears as humans in a universe. We must be aware that we are all just in an earthly way individual expressions or holograms of this energy essence in this one quantum energy field. We are formless spiritual quantum beings in a spiritual dimension having a physical body and function on frequencies. We are not separate from this energy but appear out of this energy which is beyond time, place, distance, or form. We do not need to survive because as we now know, energy can never be created or destroyed, meaning the immortal within us is timeless.

The ultimate truth of this universe is that each one of us is energy that is interconnected, entangled, and part of this one holographic existence. The oneness of this energy is all there is and nothing else. All the universe is one essence namely energy that is interconnected. The quantum energy field, consciousness, awareness, "God," Jesus, and us, are not separate or different but are all just **one eternal unlimited existence. We are the universe.** We are unlimited consciousness itself that wants to know itself as each one of us. **We are here as an**

evolving (expanding) structure inside consciousness awareness. We are all an extraordinary phenomenon of nature.

We are just spiritual divine energy (an electromagnetic field) that exists in a body. We are just spiritual beings having a human experience. Everything is energy, so energy is the source of everything and there is no separation or duality anywhere. Nikola Tesla said, "If you want to find the secrets of the universe, think in terms of energy, frequency and vibration." The physical body and mind (which is just an activity and accumulation of information) are just a temporal manifestation of this energy living as us.

Our body is a unique temporary expression, an appearance of our eternal true higher self. Our essential nature does not share the limits nor the destiny of the body and mind. In truth, we are not our mind or our body but are using it as a tool to live life and manifest our desires. We are a species in this physical world, but we are this energy field exploring itself in an environment. We are the universe (energy field), and everything is inside us.

We are here as the eternal unseen energy field (consciousness) extending into the seen to experience ourselves differently than just through an unseen field of energy. We do not enter or leave this body but are just eternal infinite vibrational energy beings, the same as a wave is part of the ocean and never leaves the ocean. The wave never leaves the ocean.

According to Dr. Joe Dispenza (a neuroscientist), we are all just distortions of this field. We are constantly collapsing in and re-emerging out of this energy field (existence) into whatever template or version we formed of ourselves (The Lamb shift). Therefore, we can evolve and change to whom we think we are and then be that new reality, and why we possess the realising power to manifest all our needs and desires within us. We can be and have anything we desire.

We really are infinite consciousness manifesting ourselves and then creating an individual and collective reality together just like a wave in the ocean that is separate from the ocean but is not. Consciousness/awareness, our essential self wants to express itself through a structure (form). Consciousness then informs itself through its designed structure (creation). Consciousness, our infinite inner being also desires to inform us what we want to know and how to accomplish all our desires.

While you as a person with a personality are changing over time, your essence as consciousness, which is your true nature never changes and is timeless. Albert Einstein said, "Energy cannot be created or destroyed, it can only be changed from one form to another." *Everything in this universe is connected as one, alive, and conscious and is just a vibration of myself.* The external universe is as much you as your own body. Nothing is ours; we are everything and that includes every being and every entity in the universe.

Enlightenment is the knowing of our own being as it really is. Enlightenment is not a goal to achieve but simply a realisation and recognition of our actual identity. *Self-knowledge is the highest form of knowledge available.* The greatest joy in the universe is self-knowledge, the revelation of who we indeed are, our true identity. This is the most important question you can ever answer and the **only basis on which to build your whole life.** We also do not need time to be who we really are. We just need to rediscover our true eternal identity again and then be that who we actually are. Rumi, a mystic, once said, *"The desire to know your own soul will end all other desires."*

The universe wants us to explore ourselves and to discover and realise that happiness is always an inside job and part of us and not dependent on happiness from the outside.

Of the most important sayings of Jesus that we tend to overlook is in John 14:20, where Jesus said, "At that moment you will know absolutely that I am in my Father, and you are in me, and I am in you." This divine energy lives in all of us, is us, and we live in it. **We are all just one**.

Beyond our body and mind, deep within us, there is a place where we are pure awareness, pure consciousness with a pure nature. Paul says in Romans 8:19, "For creation waits expectantly and longs for God's sons to be made known," meaning the universe waits to reveal to us that we are all-powerful sons (descendants, extensions) of "God" in this kingdom and **came out of this eternal godly energy field with all its privileges and powers.**

We are the greatest treasure in the world for us to find and are known by the only presence in the world that matters. We need to know who we really are. If we are a son of "God", we already are sacred, divine, whole, happy, loved, amazing, fulfilled, and valuable and do not need to become but need to just be in unity with it and be who we are. We were all created in the image or likeness of "God" with the same purity, power, perfection, joy, and infinite intelligence. We need to see our perfection and wholeness, love ourselves and just be who we actually are.

<u>**The ultimate goal in life is the self-realisation of who we really, really are.**</u> **If you think you are a material being then you will live a limited life as a material being.** We experience life as a person with a *personality* but that is not who and what we indeed are. We need to rediscover what is the value of human life, who we are and how to be who we are.

Since childhood, our personality has been forced to change to survive our circumstances and sufferings and we become someone else we are not. If we want to change our personality back to who we actually are, we need to change our old fake programmed personality which includes thinking, acting, and feeling back to that who we really are again. It is nearly impossible to transform ourselves but **when we know our true personality of who we really are, our world will change automatically without any effort or motivation from our side.** When our *personality* transforms into who we really are, our current personal reality will automatically also change simultaneously. So, we need to expand the view of who we really are and consequently will then become who we actually are. We need to transform into our true identity again. The greater our self-knowledge, the greater our joy, freedom, and happiness will be. As we will later see, it is all about our thoughts, acts, and feelings.

Essentially, we are just an extension and manifestation and not separate from this quantum energy field. The divine energy field, the spiritual dimension, wants to experience itself in all its aspects manifesting through us. Self-realisation and self-mastery are the only two components essential to living life the way you were ever meant to live. Without realising of who you really are, you will be consumed by desires and fears. To realise your actual being is the principal route to freedom and happiness which is also the basis of all Jesus' teachings and many others before and after him. Interesting to know that Jesus mainly taught what he learned from others.

Our body and mind cannot ever define or confine our true identity. It has been said that if we know our own essence or substance, then we will know the essence of everything:

1. We are **not our thoughts** (mind) because we can detach, observe, and be **aware** of our thoughts (**Thoughts are not ours** and are arising spontaneously continuously and says all sorts of things, all our life). We are also not the thinker of thoughts because the thinker of thoughts is also just a thought.
2. We are **not our emotions** (love, fear, etc.) because we can observe and be **aware** of our emotions.
3. We are **not our body** (our earth-suit) because we can observe, be **aware**, and describe our body.

We are not a human; we only think we are a human. We are not our thoughts, our emotions, or our body but the awareness or the watcher behind them. **Our thoughts, emotions and body create an apparent separate person where there is none. There is no thinker, and as said, the sense of the thinker is just another thought.** They are not the real us, but they are all just appearances, projections from our minds' perceptions. We experience ourselves as a separate person which we are, but we are not to believe in its falsehood. **The ego appears to exist when our awareness is falsely identified with thought. The ego-self (the false sense of self) pretends to be us and is very convincing.**

Our body and mind are just a flow of perceptions in consciousness, made of consciousness. Our mind and body are still consciousness, but a **limited appearance of consciousness.** The body is necessary for consciousness to taste experiences. The only thing that is real is that which never changes, namely awareness. Awareness appears in nothingness. The real us are awareness, the space within which sensations and perceptions arise. *The real us are not our mind or body but the conscious observer or awareness of our mind and body.* There is no duality although it appears as if there is. *The only thing awareness is doing is to be aware, to witness, to observe or just to be.*

CONSCIOUSNESS / AWARENESS:

You really are consciousness/awareness itself within which all experiences arise and out of which all experiences are made, and there is no reality outside consciousness. You are the space in which all things manifest and play. Awareness has got no form, but it needs the body to manifest. Consciousness is at the root of everything. You are consciousness expressing itself as a human being. You are behind the mind. You as consciousness/awareness is using the brain and mind to observe the universe. Without you being consciousness, you cannot recognise anything including any concept, thought, feeling, time- space etc. It is the same observer, awareness, and consciousness in all of us meaning we are all just one spiritual energy field, and this spiritual energy field is also part of each and every one of us. There is no existence of two powers in consciousness/awareness. Personhood then is just an appearance which then also indicates to us that our old idea of God can also not be a dualistic entity. You and I are consciousness/awareness itself and the quantum field then is in consciousness /awareness. Consciousness/awareness, which is the deepest layer uses a quantum energy field to create a world for itself and we as humans partake in it.

You need to recognise and realise that you are an aware being that is aware and essentially the presence of consciousness on earth. Consciousness/awareness is the capacity for us to have an experience. Your conscious inner awareness that you do exist is how you know you do exist. Consciousness/awareness are eternal, infinite, unlimited, formless, unlocated, unchanged and impersonal in nature. Just like the blue-sky consciousness/awareness is a state of beingness and unaffected by anything. In the light of self-awareness (self-knowing), no dysfunction or suffering can persist, meaning awareness ***does*** *not know the experience of suffering.* You are spaceless, formless awareness, and you came out of this formless awareness and are then a manifestation of this formless awareness on earth. You cannot locate yourself as awareness because you are nothing, a nobody in time and space.

Only awareness is aware and everybody and everything on earth is just one consciousness/awareness and you can directly go to this nature of yourselves. You are not really the human object but the awareness of the object, so you are really a subject or an aware being. (We are not giving it a noun which is an object, which we are not). Your body and mind (finite you) are also not you but just an object appearing or a projection within consciousness/ awareness (the infinite true you). Awareness is not the body; it functions in our body, in our earth-suit.

At the core, we are the consciousness/awareness in which all our experiences already exist. We choose our identity and body from here and what we want to experience in life. The body does not contain consciousness/awareness, the body is in consciousness/awareness, meaning there is no demarcation or boundary; otherwise, it has a form that it does not have. We as awareness are only the observer or witnesses of our thoughts, feelings, memories, perception, and sensations etc. Human beings have no awareness, only awareness has awareness. The I of the finite mind is still also the I of infinite awareness.

In the past, we learned that we first need to purify our mind (thoughts and feelings) over time before we can explore our true eternal nature. We now know this is incorrect. The direct path to the true nature of who we are is not a secret and is instantly available to anybody who wants to know who they truly are, and in fact always were. The seeing is instant for everybody but it does take time to settle the mind into this revelation or truth. Enlightenment again is the knowing of our own essential self as it really is, letting go of anything that is not part of it including our thoughts, feelings, images, perceptions, and sensations etc

We are just the infinite experiencing the finite, meaning the impermanent finite is also just an expression of consciousness. We are one quantum energy field or "God" appearing out of nothing as something. *Everybody and everything are just this energy field in disguise.* We are powerful creators who created ourselves and the whole universe. We really are unseen spiritual eternal energy beings that operate in this seen world through our mind and body but really are just an extension of this one unseen energy field in consciousness. We are just manifesting this one divine energy field.

We have a mortal mind and body but an immortal being dwells in it. The true self here is not a human being but is a quantum energy being that is everything and everywhere and will always be whole. We as the true eternal and immortal self in our wholeness need no help from outside sources. Our body, mind and emotion will die and disappear one day, but our eternal aware inner being will continue and be here for eternity. If we get rid of everything in the universe including our mind and our body, the only thing that will be left is the real conscious aware me. We go beyond time and space and are all part of this one infinite universal energy intelligence. *We really are just endless energy wrapped up in matter having sensations and then also experiences.* We cannot start exploring or changing our world if we do not recognise, realise, and accept our true identity. The fact that everybody and everything are all part of this one beingness or existence, also means that we all have the same properties of this one existing energy.

We are individual aspects, a localised electromagnetic field of this one energy field and are therefore eternal energy having an experience as a physical object or human being.

The essence of who we truly are is exactly the same as this energy field in consciousness we are living in and is one with. This means that there is a space deep within us that is timeless, formless, and spaceless and where nothing changes. We are an integral part of one complete whole.

At the core we are all from the same one essence namely energy only separated by our bodies. This is also as we now know a holographic universe so everything on the outside of us is also the same on the inside of us.

We do need to understand who and what we really are as part of and as an individualisation of this one energy field.

By realising our oneness and wholeness, we will erase any untruth. We will not need any psychotherapy or preaching to live a more divine life since we will always become whom we think we actually are.

Your true identity (nature) do include the following: You are:

Perfect, whole and divine	Timeless
Boundlessly powerful	An infinite being
Incredibly capable	Endlessly worthy
Eternal	Lackless
Changeless (unchanging)	Boundless and formless
Infinite intelligence	Consciousness itself
A son of "God"	The I am
Pure formless awareness	Existence itself
Unconditionally loved	Amazing and beautiful
Likeable and happy	A creator

- ***You are an eternal energy being.***
- You are life itself and incorruptible.
- You are the source of all manifestations.
- You are whole, complete and unpollutable.
- You are all sacred, holy, and divine.
- You are not the shape or size of your body.
- Your body is not you, but stillness appear to be movement.
- Your body is not physical, but a manifestation made from nothing.
- Your essence is beyond space and time.
- You are undefinable, meaning formless and no entity at all.
- You are connected to the source of all that is.
- You are an individualisation of one divine energy field.
- You are just a playing of this one energy, consciousness on earth, are immortal, were never born and can never die.
- Your own self is a fountain of love, kindness, and grace.
- You are love and have all goodness within. You have no beginning and no end.
- You are life and therefore cannot fade or go away. You are pure and peace itself.

- You cannot be depressed, sick, frustrated or suffer.
- You have all knowledge and wisdom.
- You have all clarity and certainty.
- Your real mind is not local.
- You are everything and are one with existence.
- You are an expression of infinity.
- You are not an idea but can only be.
- You are not a human being having consciousness, you are consciousness and awareness itself.
- You are infinite beingness, pretending to be a person.
- You are the unknowing who appears to be knowing.
- You are the infinite, experiencing the finite.
- You are the divine pretending to be ordinary.
- You are an expression of infinite awareness in which a body and this world appear. You are something appearing out of nothing.
- You are having and are aware of your earthly experiences, but you are not your experiences.
- You are one with all that is, so there is nothing you are not, cannot have and cannot be. lack nothing.
- You were not created, so you cannot fade away.
- You are the creator that creates the universe with all the creative power that has ever existed.
- You are incredibly magnificent and irreplaceable.
- You are observing change, but the real you never change.
- You are in harmony with all things - this world is not a punishment, and your body is not your enemy.
- You have no past and no future, you just are.
- You cannot be judged, there is nothing to forgive or condemn because there is nobody and nothing to judge.
- Understanding also replaces forgiveness in your mind.

The real deep down you are the whole universe.

You are the energy field from the unseen extending and manifesting itself in a physical universe and body. At our core we are an invincible source of powerful divine energy.

You cannot see who you are because you are not a thing. Your true self is before thoughts and emotions began.

Even to say I or I am can be wrong because we cannot describe our real nature. I am is an object (entity), and there is no object (entity) at the core of this energy field.

You are not in a physical world, the physical world is in you, meaning I is not in your body, your body is in I. What you experience is not at all who you are. You are not really particles but are localised waves of energy interacting with others.

I really do think that deep down we all know this is true knowledge, but some of us have not stopped to acknowledge it.

ONENESS:
Ultimately, the entire universe experience takes place inside us. ***We were this energy field before we came into this world.*** We need to truly know that we are *one* with a powerful energy field and are just an extension and manifestation of it. All then is one, and one is all there is, it is everything. Everybody and everything are indeed just us, I am you and you are me, we are one.

We are all eternally connected to that which we are. We need to realise that everybody is *one* and entangled and just an extension and part of this *one* godly energy field manifesting into the seen physical world. We really are this *one* energy field manifesting as world citizens, meaning the world is not separate from us. If we had not lost our true identity, we would have known that there is a place where we are inseparable and *one* with this powerful godly energy field. The same powerful energy that moves the oceans exists within us.

We are the timeless experiencing time, the formless experiencing form, the pure experiencing imperfection, and the imperishable experiencing mortality. As we know by now, we are all divine, powerful, infinite beings. The divine energy field is here within us and flows through us. The real self of man is divine energy and can do anything. There is then no you outside this divine energy field.

In the end, nothing but nothing will satisfy or make you happy including all the riches in the world until you realise who you really are, then you will be entirely free. When you know your true identity, then and only then will you be fully free and then everything will satisfy you.

The divine purpose of this universal energy field then is really to know itself through the realisation of our formless essence or substance and through the creation of form. Although love, us, our thoughts, emotions, things etc. are only vibrational frequencies, we can experience it differently than just only through an unseen quantum field of energy. This means the energy field wants to become conscious of itself through us and experience itself by materialising as form.

We are a species in this physical world but in reality, we are this energy field that is exploring an environment. *We are the eyes through which this energy field looks at the universe.* What we experience and feel is what the energy field is experiencing and feeling. We are also co-creating with this one creative energy field within.

We are creators because we have a mind and a body with emotions that causes feelings that have creative power.

According to our feelings, the heart radiates an electromagnetic force into our body causing atoms to change within and also radiates information out into the electromagnetic energy field around us.

The good news is that this divine energy field is in us and flows through us in all its love, joy, peace, and happiness.

If we know who we really are and that we are holy and divine and do not doubt these truths, we will automatically want and be willing to change without being forced into it. *If we really know who we are, the purifying of our old selves will really be effortless and without resistance. This power will be awakened and be resurrected in us.* The power source within us will rise up and become alive. If you really know who you are, you will heal your internal and also your external life. We will then be able to permanently be transformed, instead of just improving ourselves.

OUR PERSONALITY / IDENTITY:

What personality we identify with will determine the nature of our thoughts, emotions, behaviour, and beliefs and therefore our personal reality. Everything that happens in our reality is going to happen to uphold the identity of whom we think we are. Whom we think we are (our personal identity) is how we see and then create things in our life. Our identity or personality creates our personal reality. We can only attract according to the true picture in our mind of whom we think we are as a person. We can only create and manifest out of our idea of our personality (our mind with its thoughts, acts, and feelings) and not anything else.

We do now know that our true personality is whole, holy, and divine. Our old personality in our subconscious mind is just a defensive cover or overlay over who we truly are, a mechanism to survive, cope and to keep us safe until we can discover our own true identity, our true self, which will then replace that. Our subconscious mind is always only busy protecting us for survival. Our old personal identity is connected to our past and really is just a fake identity or self-construct, an appearance that is not permanent and which we can change. Our current reality is a direct reference to our personality or the identity we have currently of ourselves. We need to break the habit of being our old personality, our old identity, or old self with its behaviours and change our state of being to the real us.

It takes a long time for us to change our own ego identity with our mind. However, if we truly know ourselves as awareness, we will effortlessly activate or manipulate the circuits in the brain to change into a new personality. As mentioned before, our success is a side effect of who we truly are.

We cannot train or desire to be ourselves, we just need to be who we truly already are, and our old personality will effortlessly change. We need to take back our real divine behaviour pattern. We cannot change our fundamental nature, but if we can change our old personality of whom we think we are to our true identity of who we really are, everything will happen. If we know who we really are, we rewire the connections in our brain and send new electrochemical message to our body, and our personality will change. We will then attract according to the new construct of who we really are into our personal reality.

If we know our true identity and personality and know that we are eternal creators and co-creators of this creation, we have got a formula to change our personal reality. Our personal reality is then a mirror that reflects our attitude, either positive or negative towards us. Our true personality and inner higher self, need to be ideally in unity in action, thought and emotion for the ideal personal reality to happen, and this is what we will examine.

Knowing and loving ourselves is the most powerful self-healing power and part of the ultimate truth of oneness. If we know our true divine identity, we will love ourselves. Self-love is just a celebration of us knowing who we truly are. To love ourselves is to love everything else also. When we love ourselves, we are one with the universe and able to love everybody else and create anything we desire. We are whole, worthy, valuable, and perfect so we must be proud of ourselves and never dwell on thoughts of who we are not. True happiness is causeless and within us. The opposite is also true that if we do not actually understand who we really are, we will not want to, or will not be able to change which will cause guilt and an inability to manifest our own desires.

IMPORTANCE OF WORTHINESS:
Your view of worthiness significant impacts your thoughts and what you will be able to attract and create in your life. If you understand that you are this eternal energy field and were always whole, how will you ever feel guilty or condemned and thus disable your creative ability? If you do not know who you really are, doubt kicks in which blocks your feeling of worthiness, which then blocks the creation of your specific desires. You will also later see that if you do not live an authentic life with honesty and integrity, you will be doubtful in your own mind, not trust yourself and then not feel worthy to receive your

creation. Experiencing unworthiness or guilt will cause an inability to create the ideal life. Our thoughts will also be disorganised if we are not living with integrity an honest, sincere, and authentic life.

If you really know that you are beautiful, whole, and divine, you will want to live accordingly and purify your life and then attract that who you are. If you know who you actually are with all these truths, you will not need any psychotherapy or preaching of any kind, and the following emotions and feelings will *disappear effortlessly:*

Stress	Fear
Anxiety	Anger
Hate	Depression
Competition	Selfishness
Judgement	Condemnation
Bitterness	Struggle
Strife	Lying etc.

You are a separate identity inside a physical body. You are this energy field, so all perfection and every divine virtue are hidden within you, and you reveal them to the world through your way of living. You are not your past, your mind, or your body, you were here before birth and will be here after you die. The truth of who you really are cannot be named, cannot be defined, cannot be thought, is untouched by any concept of who you really are, and can also never really be satisfactorily answered. In the end, when your body and mind (finite part) die, you will just re-emerge into this eternal (infinite) energy field. At the end there is no entity at all but only this infinite boundless existence. Rather than just being a quantum energy field, the universe is experiencing and uniquely knowing itself while it manifests and expands.

You are eternal and an incredible, powerful, magnificent, perfect, and unique expression of the infinite. You are here to come together as a physical and a spiritual being. The more your higher inner being, your mind and your body come together, the more you will enjoy this world and experience happiness and heaven on earth. All is well, and you cannot attain who you already are. Happiness and perfection are your true nature. Salvation (deliverance of your problems on earth) and freedom lies inside you where the power of all and everything is. You can now love yourself.

The separate self is just a mental construct. If you believe in personhood, then you believe in separation (dualism), which you understand is not rational thinking anymore. There is no individual person inside you and no "God" outside of you. There is nothing but this infinite godly quantum energy field. Our old beliefs as a person come from what other people, family, religion, culture, friends, or history, etc. tells us. Our old beliefs can cause us to be filled with hatred, anger, judgement, condemnation, fear, anxiety, and stress instead of love and happiness. These emotions block our manifestations from experiencing a happy, abundant, and fulfilled life.

Salvation means to saving yourself from your own misunderstandings about life and how it functions, your wholeness and who you really are. The past will lose all its meaning because all the past pain only happened to our old concept of self. If you know who you really are you will have self-love and therefore be satisfied with yourself and others, and the reason for any judgement and negative emotions with suffering will also disappear.

You cannot train or desire to be yourself, you just need to be yourself. If you really know that you are whole, holy and an expression of the divine, you will not need to clean or discipline yourself but only require clarity of what is not. There is no emotional trip needed down memory lane and you will not need any healing, you just need to **be who you truly are**. The infinite aware you do not know suffering, sickness, or death. You are whole, amazing, loveable, noble, and always worthy to receive all of your desires. You need to repent and change your mind concerning your true identity of whom you think you really are, and out of that, you will experience the following feelings permanently:

Love	Freedom
Peace	Happiness
Gratefulness	Gratitude Appreciation
Compassion Ecstasy	Bliss

You will then be totally free and will also realise that you are not here to:
- fix or solve something,
- do, undo or control something,
- accomplish, learn a lesson or achieve something,
- be or change to become somebody,
- be better than anybody,
- worry about anything,
- compete with anybody or to win any prize, it is not a game fulfill an individual plan or goal,
- save or redeem anybody, and there is no judge and no trial.
- There is also nothing to construct or to break down.
- ***You do not need to fulfil any purpose.***
- ***You do not have any destiny.***
- ***You are not on any spiritual path or spiritual journey.***

There is nothing to get out of life, there is only you and you are life and also the witness of life. The real you are not a somebody which life pushes around. The real deep down you are the whole universe. You do not need to earn anything, and you are complete.

You came for the joy of being here, to experience life, not for any results. It is not a game you need to play or a competition you need to win, you are just here to play. Your body is the instrument through which consciousness can taste diverse experiences and impact the universe. We are not material beings but dimensional beings having dimensional experiences and need to become in harmony with who we really are. There is no way to absolutely say what our higher self in this reality is because, it ultimately transcends human language and conceptualisation. The perfection of who you are is also continuously expanding meaning you are constantly evolving as an earthly being. You are not moving from imperfection to perfection, but from perfection to perfection.

You are the source of all that is, and you came here to manifest yourself. ***The body and mind we are living in is only a transient (finite) experience, and we do not need them to exist.*** In the spiritual world you are one aware being but, in this world, you have the appearance of being solid. Your natural state is abundance since you create your own reality. The evidence of your spirituality will show up in your physical world as material stuff. If you genuinely know who you really are, you will be able to create all your desires and whatever you want to experience.

Only be here, be present, enjoy and love yourself and know how magnificent and powerful you already are.

We need to know there is not something like a physical body. We are not made of anything physical, that is just a human concept, an appearance. Humans are just an extension of this divine energy field, a manifestation or individualisation of this divinity. We are just the invisible appearing to be visible, the timeless appearing in time. We are all aspects of godliness, and there is no separation between us. A person is just a limited construction with a finite personality (a mask), with a beginning and an end.

THE KNOWLEDGE WITHIN:
Science says 99.999 percent of every atom made from proton particles in your body only consists of empty space filled with energy that is vibrating, then meaning 99.999 percent of your body is just empty space and the 0.111 percent of mass, is also just energy vibrating at a specific frequency. *We are not really a solid object, entity, or thing but mostly just an empty space (spaceless).* Space and time are constants to create an environment in which we can play and have linear experiences in.

All the information in the universe is in its totality in every single proton particle in existence. Each proton particle is being networked to nearly every other proton particle through entanglement. We are made of these linked proton particles which means that every single proton in your body has all the information of the universe in it and is continuously getting updated by being connected to each other. All your answers for guidance then remain within yourself in every single proton. The thought you are thinking right now, as you will see later, is impacting every one of the 50-100 trillion atoms in each cell of the 50-100 trillion cells in your body and at quantum speed.

Proteins are responsible for the structure and function of your body. Your body is made from 150 000 different proteins consisting of atoms containing proton, neutron and electron particles vibrating in waves together forming a localised interacting energy field controlled by the electromagnetic forces. Every cell in our body is bathed in an external and internal environment of a fluctuating electromagnetic field. This electromagnetic field then affects every atom vibration in every protein molecule in your life. These atoms with their protons, absorb energy and radiate, giving off energy. Fluctuations in this magnetic field influence every atom and therefore every protein in your body. Our bodies are then really just made of everchanging interacting fields of energy. *When you change the energy field an atom lives in your body, you change the atom which then changes the body.*

By changing your thought of what you desire, you are changing your emotion and then *forming a new feeling which changes the energy frequency that you are sending* or broadcasting into the surrounded electromagnetic field. As said, if you change the field, you change the body and then attract a new experience. The new experience will be attracted towards you by you attracting the same energy and experience as the feeling of the desire you have radiated into the field.

THOUGHTS, EMOTIONS AND FEELINGS:
There is a significant difference between our emotions and our feelings, and it is crucially important to differentiate between the two of them. The creative energy field did create thoughts, emotions, and feelings through evolution as a way to help us to manage our own lives. Our whole life is just thoughts, emotions, feelings, and actions. Your **thoughts** and **emotions** in your body effects the *feelings* you are having, and the feelings then will influence your whole personal reality. We will discuss this later in detail but here are the basics.

THOUGHTS:
Thinking thoughts formed as part of the evolution proses. Thinking came into existence as a way for us to achieve what we desire. Your thoughts will determine your reality. Remember, you are not the thinker of your thoughts and feelings, so do not believe everything you think.

Thoughts are not ours and are arising spontaneously continuously in consciousness and say all sorts of things all your life. They often arise from memories from the old, programmed subconscious mind, but also from other sources, e.g., your DNA, news etc. You need to only see them for what they are. ***You are separate from your thoughts and can control your thoughts and emotions to create or manifest your own reality.***

A thought on its own also has got no power or importance and is really just a ***memory that recycles itself***. However, a specific thought can influence and change our emotion and then our feelings which then change the vibration of our magnetic field. Any thought needs an emotion from you to become a reality in life. This will then influence the energy in the electromagnetic field in your body and around you, then attract a new experience. So, when you give a thought attention with an emotion, it will become an experience.

Not all your wanting thoughts coming into your conscious mind from the subconscious mind needs attention, so you need never just follow them blindly but need to control them. Do not believe in everything you think. ***Your thoughts are meant to be controlled by you***, so do not let junk thoughts from outside sources enter your mind. If you do not like the thought entering your mind, you are free and need to change your attention to another thought you do like.

We are all just vibrational beings, and the thoughts we are thinking influence the emotion (high or low) and then the level of the vibration of the energy field we are in. The energy level in the measurable magnetic field can increase or decrease according to our emotions. If you are in an elevated emotion, ***a high-speed vibrational frequency*** you are confident with a powerful sense of trust to create. If you are in a ***low-speed vibration frequency,*** you are in doubt and will not be able to create.

Your consciousness, awareness, perception, and knowledge are also heightened if you are in a state of high-speed vibration, and you will experience greater personal power, clarity, peace, love, and joy. Your best feeling thought with a strong emotion will bring you to the highest frequency vibration and then the best results. So, you always need to think about the thoughts that give you the best feeling. Your thoughts can only affect your own emotional vibrational frequency and therefore only your own outcome and personal reality.

EMOTIONS:
There are about eight basic emotions in life. These are trust (love), fear, sadness, disgust, surprise, anger, anticipation, and joy. *The two most important basic opposite energies at the core of the human emotional experience are love (trust) and fear (distrust),* with then all other emotional energies between these two emotions. Your current emotions are only a residue of the past, and if you do not actively change them, they will not change.

THOUGHTS AND EMOTIONS:
Only the thoughts you make active by attaching an emotion can affect or influence you. Any thought and an added emotion in the body will form a feeling that has creative or manifesting power. The thought-feeling will send a specific vibrational frequency message into the electromagnetic field and attract the same energy and experience as the feeling that was radiated.

FEELINGS:
<u>Feelings were in the evolution proses over time replaced by language as a method of communicating (interacting) and creating in this universe</u>. A feeling is a vibration of energy at a specific frequency tied with specific information carrying a specific thought or message into the universe. There are hundreds of different positive (pleasant) and negative (unpleasant) feelings including the following, a feeling of abundance, love, happiness, sadness, fear or worry, etc. There is an infinite number of thought-feelings. Feelings are magnetic in nature, and a specific energy frequency will attract (pull) similar energy like a magnet according to the strength of the feeling towards itself. Your feelings manifest the destiny you want, and a change of a feeling is a change of your destiny. It works for all feelings, every time and for everybody.

Everything in nature communicates with feelings (energy vibrations). This then means we also need to be sensitive about our feelings towards anything and everybody for the reason that that is the language of the universe.

We as humans are really just interacting waves (not particles or matter) emitting vibrations which is why one person can affect another by being in their vibrating electromagnetic field. So, we need to be sensitive to the vibrations radiating toward us from other people.

Your body is an organised region of energy and just an extension of the unseen energy field and has a particular set of information or coding. By causing specific emotions in the body, you can influence it and change the energy in its electromagnetic field and therefore what the field emits.

The heart's electromagnetic field contains information or coding that researchers are still trying to understand fully. Intentionally generated emotions can change this information or coding and it is then that this magnetic field change influences our bodies and everything around us.

There are an infinite number of thought-feeling patterns and therefore an infinite number of frequencies of this energy vibrating. Different thought-feelings have different vibration frequencies and there are an infinite number of frequencies. A frequency (Hz units) is the rate at which vibrations and oscillations occur (vibration x cycles per second). Frequencies are used to determine and differentiate between vibrational patterns (thoughts).

Thus, frequencies distinguish between different information or messages which will be radiating into the electromagnetic field and universe, possibly into eternity.

The energy level in the measurable magnetic field can also increase or decrease according to our emotions. The higher the emotion the faster the frequency of energy vibration and the stronger the power of the magnetic attraction. The strength of the dominant feeling then is the power for the desire to manifest. This magnetic attraction works continuously (always) for everybody on earth.

Ultimately all nature is just vibrations of energy at different frequencies of various underlying energy fields, meaning everything has got a vibrational frequency. The electromagnetic field is not affected by an **electrical thought** alone, but only by the strength of an added elevated emotion, forming a **magnetic field,** and then together forming a feeling (an electromagnetic field). All things in our universe are constantly in motion, vibrating. **Vibration refers to the oscillating and vibrating movement of particles caused by energy**. Even objects that appear stationary are in fact vibrating, oscillating and resonating at various frequencies.

Everything you ask for is already coming to you. You attract anything and everything you are in harmony or alignment with, **good or bad.** A specific feeling is a specific energy vibration that will attract a similar energy vibration like a magnet according to the strength of the feeling towards itself. Your emotions for example fear or trust, are an indicator of your energy vibration. The more positive you feel, the more you trust, the closer you are getting to wholeness or oneness, the faster the frequency of the vibration will be and vice versa. Trusting, causing a positive emotion radiates a high energy vibration, and worry, causing a negative emotion will radiate low energy vibration. The higher (faster) the frequency of your energy or vibration, the lighter you feel in your physical, emotional, and mental state.

The feeling of worry (fear) is the biggest killer of all our dreams and desires, whereas the feeling of trust is the surest way of fulfilling them. We need to live a life of trust and not of worry. Remember what happened to Job from the Old Testament, the things that he feared came over him. We can now stand without fear or worry because of who we really are as a creator.

We do need to reinvent ourselves. We need to be ourselves knowingly. The more we know and become who we really already are, the more we will detach from our own opinion of who we are and the less we will fear our own power. The essence of our mind is intrinsically pure, but every idea, every thought, every emotion, and every value that we have, is picked up from somewhere, and it rules within us. The brain is just a record or artefact of the past. Although the content of our brain/mind is not our choice it is still useful, and we can always change anything we desire with our true feelings.

THE ELECTROMAGNETIC FIELD OF THE HEART:

The heart is a creative centre. By changing the knowledge of who we indeed are, we are changing the electromagnetic field of the heart which will electromagnetically change our body and due to entanglement, radiate into everything in and around us. The electromagnetic field in and around the body's heart emits signals into our body and the universe that affects us and the whole universe. The quantum energy field only recognises the electromagnetic waves through the power of the heart and not through the voice or words of the person. We can change the atom electrically known as the Zeeman effect, or magnetically known as the Stark effect. The heart is 60 times more electrically charged than the brain, and the heart is 100 times more magnetically charged than the brain. In 1991, Dr Andrew Armour discovered a tiny little brain (intrinsic nervous system) in our heart consisting of 40 thousand sensory neurites (neurons like the brain) that function independently from the brain. This little brain acts independently of the brain, sending and receiving meaningful messages of its own through the autonomic nervous system. The heart's little brain works in two diverse ways. It can act in harmony with the brain as a single unit or independently of the brain where it can think, remember, learn, and even sense our inner and outer worlds on its own. This will be discussed later but we need to harmonise our brain and body to affect our hearts electromagnetic field.

The ultimate way of raising your energy vibration to the highest level and releasing all resistance is by being appreciative of who you really are, the truth that you are a creator, holy and divine. The highest form of vibration is having the true knowledge of who you really are. You need to tune into the energy frequency of who you really are, and then then everything else will take care of itself. Whom you are and understanding your energy vibrational level of consciousness is one of the most crucial factors for successful living in this universe.

By recognising who you really are, you raise your vibration and will have whatever you desire. This is all then a side effect of who you really are. You also need to have the specific quality yourself before you attract the specific wanted desire. You need to become a vibrational match to your desire, and then you will attract what you put out in this quantum energy field.

Doing things from the basis of who and what you really are will have the most creative power. You need to be the way you really are and identify with that new version and change your thoughts, feelings, and emotions accordingly.

You need to listen to your eternal inner higher self that will lead you to all the knowledge you will ever need in life. Entertain only feelings that will contribute to your joy and happiness. The stronger the feeling entertained, the stronger the field will be and then the stronger the attraction towards you will be. As we will later see, you need to simply decide what and who you are, then visualise it, and then think, feel, and act accordingly.

Be aware of your old self and its patterns but know that that is not the truth of who you now know you are. At the lower level of vibration, you are trying to have things that cause satisfaction only in the short term.

Nothing but nothing will give you long-term satisfaction in this world until you realise who you really are, and then, and then only will you get permanent satisfaction in what you manifest. "As a man thinketh, so is he." All self-worth problems come from our idea that we think that we are not enough. You are not ordinary as you learned in the past, you are beautiful and extraordinary. You were created as a true image of "God." "God" is man, and man is "God," there are no two beings.

You have not been born in sin but were born beautiful, whole, and complete. You are special, sacred, holy, worthy, and loved. You are already whom you need to be, and you are not to become, you are. The past has no effect on your present except as much as you put trust or believe in it. You are allowed to have self-love because that is just a celebration and recognition of the knowledge that you know your true identity of who you actually are. As you will see later, now that you know who you really are, you can create your own reality deliberately. You used to create entirely from your ego-mind (false sense of self). However, once you know who you really are, your true identity, you can stop creating from the temporal (finite) self and start creating from the eternal (infinite) higher self, intentionally through the temporal self.

If you are fully confident of who you are and doubtless in your choice, your creation will always happen. Through stillness and meditation, you can decide your purpose in life, as well as how you will be fulfilled.

It is also the practice of stillness meditation that will enable you to create out of your higher self and not from your ego.

Now that you know who you really are, you know that you are a powerful creator and can create your own reality. You now know you are an extension of the energy field and embedded with the same powerful creative energy. You are quantum energy in a physical body and the energy field does not hear your words but your thoughts and feelings. The only connection between you and the energy field is through your feelings (thoughts and emotions). You are also causing an expansion of the quantum energy field with every feeling-thought you are thinking.

You are separate from your thoughts and can control your thoughts and emotions to create or manifest your own reality.

Our true essence (as energy) is beyond space and time, but space and time are constructs to create an environment for us to have a linear experience, a place for us to play in and experience where our dominant thoughts and feeling attracts similar events, people etc.

We all are just part of one functional energy field.

So, the quantum energy field will work for us as us to create according to our feelings, whether it is good or bad. If we understand who is the real me, and if we understand these fundamentals, all other things will fall in place for us.

Through stillness and meditation, we can discover how to be in harmony and alignment with this energy field which is our highest call and the best way of living.

There are ways and laws of doing things in every kingdom on earth, and there are also ways and laws of doing things in this energy field, realm, or kingdom we live in. We do need to understand its laws and its ways of doing things to live in it successfully. **Firstly, we need to understand who we really are in this kingdom (energy field) otherwise we will feel insecure and condemned and will not be able to live freely and manifest effectively.** In the end, there really is only this one energy field or kingdom that we are all a part of, there is only one energy field, but not everybody knows of its existence and its creative power.

How you exactly feel in your heart indicates what will happen to you. As a man thinks in his heart, his true feelings or all that man achieves is the direct result of his own thoughts, so he is, and as he continues to think, so he remains. As you think, so shall you be. **The more worthy you feel, the more magnetic you become for abundance.** If you think wrong, you will create wrong, every time.

You cannot change the world while you are staying the same but by changing the way how you think and feel, you reprogram your subconscious mind effortlessly into the real you. If you want to see your future and what and where you will be, just look at your thoughts about it. Your own vision is what you one day shall be and have. Whom you think you are as a person (your identity) is how you look at things in your life. **Who you really already are and understanding your vibrational level of consciousness is one of the most crucial factors for successful living in this universe. Seeing the image of godliness in yourself and that you are one with the universe and one with all people will raise your vibration because this is again who you really are.** The greatest gift we can give our children is to allow them to be who they are and let them go in the direction that they feel about going instead of us dictating to them where they should go. They need also to understand that they are far more powerful than they have ever been taught.

You are already everything you are searching for, nothing can be added or taken away from you. You need to understand that your manifestations and experiences are just to aid you to realise you are already everything you are looking for on the inside and will not need anything on the outside to be more content, and also to help you in the expansion of your consciousness. You are just existence announcing itself. Anything you manifest and experience will and cannot give you lasting satisfaction. **No experience can bring you permanent happiness until you know who you indeed are, then everything will make you peaceful and happy.** You create your own reality, so if you arrange your mind, then happiness is something you can decide on in advance or ahead of time. The world appears out of you which means that you can control your own destiny. There are also an infinite amount of quantum energy, therefore infinite health, wealth, and abundance available for you. You always need to be abundant in your awareness, knowing that everything is available for you.

These universal principles are reflected in many spiritual teachings. What has long been thought to be just the wisdom of spiritual men (Sages, Jesus, mystics, yogis, gurus, Buddha) has now been proven to be a reality in the findings of quantum science, the science of possibilities.

I really believe that these following two spiritual teachings are so scientific that they will be the standard way of living in time to come. It will stop being just spiritual teachings and become the normal scientific way of how life operates.

Here we will now see the biblical (spiritual, mystical) truth that we are all holy, sacred, divine, and amazing and filled with unlimited spiritual creative power to manifest abundance in all the areas (body and mind) of our life.

LUKE 4:14-32 (NKJ): Self-realisation – All the power is within us

Then Jesus returned in **the power of the Spirit** to Galilee, and news of Him went out through all the surrounding regions.[15] And He taught in their synagogues, being glorified by all.[16] So He came to Nazareth,

where He had been brought up. And as His custom was, He went into the synagogue on the Sabbath day, and stood up to read.[17] And He was handed the book of the prophet Isaiah. And when he opened the book, **he found the place where it was written,**[18] **"The Spirit of the LORD is upon Me,**
Because **He has anointed Me**
To preach the gospel to *the* **poor;**
He has sent Me to heal the **broken hearted**,
To proclaim liberty to *the* **captives**
And recovery of sight to *the* **blind**,
To set at liberty those who are **oppressed**;
[19] To proclaim the acceptable year of the LORD."[20] Then He closed the book and gave *it* back to the attendant and sat down. And the eyes of all who were in the synagogue were fixed on Him.[21] And He began to say to them, **"Today this Scripture is fulfilled in your hearing."**[22] So all bore witness to Him and marvelled at the gracious words which proceeded out of His mouth. And they said, "Is this not Joseph's son?"

[23] He said to them, "You will surely say this proverb to Me, 'Physician, heal yourself! Whatever we have heard done in Capernaum, do also hear in Your hometown. Then he said, Assuredly, I say to you, no prophet is accepted in his hometown.[25] But I tell you truly, many widows were in Israel in the days of Elijah, when the heaven was shut up three years and six months, and there was a great famine throughout all the land;[26] but to none of them was Elijah sent except to Zarephath, *in the region* of Sidon, to a woman *who was* a widow.[27] And many lepers were in Israel in the time of Elisha the prophet, and none of them was cleansed except Naaman the Syrian."

[28] So all those in the synagogue, when they heard these things, were filled with wrath,[29] and rose up and thrust Him out of the city; and they led Him to the brow of the hill on which their city was built, that they might throw Him down over the cliff.[30] Then passing through the midst of them, He went His way.[31] Then He went down to Capernaum, a city of Galilee, and was teaching them on the Sabbaths.[32] **And they were astonished at His teaching, for His word was with authority.**

Verse 32

Here, Luke tells us that this was Jesus' teaching or doctrine. If you have faith and are a follower of Jesus, then his teachings must be especially important to you. If you say you are a follower of Jesus, you need to investigate what his doctrines were because that was what was important to him. Many of us can quote Jesus' sayings, but who really knows his doctrines or teachings? *Jesus had mainly two teachings that the bible calls his teachings or doctrines.* He was preaching many times in the gospels and the people were astonished, but what were his fundamental doctrines?

Verse 18

Jesus read the book of the prophet Isaiah 61:1, now exactly repeated in Luke 4:18. Isaiah 61:1 reads, "The Spirit of the Lord God is upon me because the Lord hath anointed me to preach good tidings unto the meek; he hath send me to bind up the broken-hearted, to proclaim the liberty to the captives, and the opening of the prison to them that are bound."

He agrees that the spirit of "God" is in him (he is filled with powerful energy), and he is anointed (smeared) with this power of "God" (powerful energy was smeared on him). We can see that Jesus the man discovered that he was aware of this divine energy power, and he was filled and anointed himself. So, what does the spirit or *powerful energy of "God"* do, and why is it so important that he was saying that the Spirit of the Lord is upon him and that he was anointed. We need to find a definition of *anointing*. In Isaiah 10:27 we read, "And it shall come to pass in that day that his burden shall be taken away from off thy shoulder and his yoke from off thy neck and the *yoke shall be destroyed because of the anointing."*

Anointing then means burden removing and yoke destroying power of "God." A yoke is a kind of harness that is used for oxen to get them to pull a card or farming equipment which was heavy and difficult to carry, typically one yoke for two oxen. *A yoke figuratively then can be used for severe bondage, subjection, or affliction.* Now Jesus is telling his followers that the *power of the Holy Spirit* rests on him with this burden removing, yoke destroying energy power. Stating that this *powerful energy (anointing)* can heal anybody who has problems in any area of their life on this earth, and that includes the whole you (mind and body), meaning nothing but nothing in you experiencing life abundantly will be left out. This *creative powerful energy* will not just break but will destroy anything that prevents us from living in abundance. *Destroy means cannot ever be put back together again.*

Verse 21
Here, Jesus Christ accepts the fact he was also anointed and filled with this power of the Lord, as Isaiah was. According to the covenant in Isaiah 59:21, everybody else has also been filled with this *powerful spiritual energy*. Isaiah 59:21 says, "This is my covenant promise with them," says Lord Yahweh. "From now on my *Holy Spirit (my powerful energy)* will rest on them and not depart from them and my prophetic words will fill their mouths and will not depart from them, nor from their children, nor their *descendants, from now on and forever."* (The Passion Translation)

In 1 John 2:20, talking about us, we read, "But you have been anointed by the Holy One and you know all things." *Here we see that the same powerful spiritual energy that was within Jesus was accepted to abide in us also.* As Jesus was, we also have been *anointed* (covered, filled) with this yoke destroying powerful energy by the Holy One. In 1 John 2:27 we read. "But the *anointing* which ye have received of him abides in you."

We now know and we need to realise that we are all covered and filled with this same *powerful creative universal energy* and there is no difference between the essence of *Jesus' power* and the essence of ours. The quality and strength of *Jesus' power is* exactly the same as yours. This has now also been proven by current scientific evidence, proving that the universe consists of *powerful creative energy*.

Verse 31
If we follow the teachings of Jesus after his reading in the synagogue, we will discover that *Jesus and his followers' main teaching was about this powerful energy (anointing) in the "Kingdom of God," which they then demonstrated with miracles.* The people were amazed as I

was amazed to discover this creative and powerful energy (anointing) inside, among and available to all of us. ***This was the message that Jesus asked his followers to take to the rest of the world.*** This news and nothing else were the good news or gospel Jesus wanted to teach us.

THE KINGDOMS POWER IS WITHIN US – JESUS

Every kingdom is beneficial if you know you belong to it. ***We will now see that the knowledge of this power of the Kingdom of God inside and among us has been taught by Jesus Christ and all his followers,*** convincing everybody that with this powerful energy (anointing), everyone can live in abundance in all areas of their lives.

Luke 4:43 (Jesus preach)
And he said unto them, ***I must preached the kingdom of God to other cities also: for therefore am I sent***

Luke 8:1 (Jesus preach)
And it come to past afterward, that he went throughout every city and village, preaching and shewing the ***glad tidings of the kingdom of God:*** and the twelve were with him,

Luke 9:2 (Twelve apostles preach)
And he sent them to preach the ***kingdom of God,*** and to heal the sick.

Luke 9:11 (Jesus preach)
And the people, when they knew it, followed him: and he received them ,and spoke unto them of the ***kingdom of God***, and healed them that had need healing.

Luke 9:27 (Jesus preach)
But I tell you of a truth, there be some standing here, ***which shall not taste death, till they see the kingdom of God***

Luke 9:60 (Jesus preach)
Jesus said unto them ,Let the dead bury their dead: but go thou and preach the ***kingdom of God.***

Luke 10:9 (Seventy disciples preach)
And heal the sick that are therein, and say unto them, The **kingdom of God** is come nigh unto you.

Luke 12:31 (Jesus preach)
But rather seek ye the **kingdom of God**; and all these things shall be added unto you.

Luke 16:16 (Luke wrote)
The law and the prophets were until John: since that time the kingdom of God is preached, and every man presses into it.

Luke 18:17 (Jesus preach)
Verily I say unto you, whosoever shall not receive the **kingdom of God** as a little child shall in no wise enter therein.

Luke 18:25 (Jesus preach)
For it is easier for a camel to go through a needle's eye, than for a rich man to enter into the **kingdom of God**.

John 3:3 (Jesus preach)
Jesus answered and said unto him, Verily, verily, I say unto thee, ***Except a man born again, he cannot see the kingdom of God.***

Acts1:3 (Jesus preaching)
To whom also he shewed himself alive after his passion by many infallible proofs, being seen of them forty days, and speaking of the things pertaining to the **kingdom of God:**

Acts 8:12 (Philip preaching)
But when they believed Philip preaching the things concerning the **kingdom of God**, and the name of Jesus Christ, they were baptized, both men and women.

Acts 19:8 (Paul preaching)
And he went into the synagogue, and spoke boldly for the space of three months, disputing and persuading the things concerning the **kingdom of God**.

Act 20:8 (Paul preaching)
And now, behold, I know that ye all, among whom I have gone preaching the **kingdom of God**, shall see my face no more.

Acts 18:31 (Paul preaching)
Preaching the **kingdom of God**, and teaching those things which concern the Lord Jesus Christ, with all confidence, no man forbidding him.

1 Cor 2:4 (Paul preaching)
And my speech and my preaching was not with enticing words of man's wisdom, but in the demonstration of the Spirit and of power;

1 Cor 4:20 (Paul preaching)
For **the kingdom of God is not in word, but in power.**

Ephesians 6:10 (Unknown)
Finally my brethren, be strong in the Lord, and in the power of his might.

Acts 2:22 (Luke wrote?)
"Men of Israel, listen to these words: Jesus of Nazareth, a Man accredited *and* pointed out *and* attested to you by God with [the power to perform] **miracles and wonders and signs which God worked through Him in your [very] midst**, just as you yourselves know."

Here we can see that the core message of all of Jesus Christ and his followers was to bring the knowledge of this powerful creative energy of the kingdom of "God" within and around us to everybody on earth. Jesus came here to open our eyes to show us that "God" and his power are also in us. Jesus's revelation to us was that of our divine sonship. Jesus and his disciples also demonstrated that it was real with miracles and that it was available here and now. If you follow all their sermons, you will discover that they were nearly always followed by miracles to demonstrate that this power that breaks the yokes was real and immediately available for those who understood (comprehend) this knowledge and also the reality and availability of this power. Sometimes it was the other way around, and miracles would first happen to demonstrate this power, and then the good news of this kingdom of God and its creative power was preached. In Acts 2:22, we read that God worked through Jesus, meaning Jesus was used to demonstrating this powerful energy.

Christ is not Jesus' surname, but christ is a description of an intrinsic creative energy power within us.

The word christ comes from 'christos,' a Greek word meaning anointed. It is the equivalent of the Hebrew word mashiach (messiah). The word **christ means the anointed one (the person that is filled with power) and his anointing (the power he is filled with).** Paul in Cor 1:27 says, *"which is christ (the creative power) within and among you,* the hope of glory (to success)."

While reading out of the book Isaiah, Jesus understood that he was explicitly filled with this creative power (anointed) and also understood what this power was for. He recognised that "christ" (the divine creative energy, spirit of God) was within him, meaning this powerful energy of God was within to be used to regulate his life.

We need to realise now that we are also all filled with this same power biblically and scientifically. In 1 John 2:20 talking about us, we read, ***"But you have been anointed (covered) by the Holy One, and you know all things."*** We all have been filled with this same holy and divine power and hence are also Christ's (Christians) and need to live accordingly. The Bible often speaks about christ within us, meaning this endless powerful energy within to be used to reclaim (salvage) and regulate our own life.

We also know we have all the knowledge within that there ever was and ever will be. Jesus, after he again recognised that this creative power (spirit) was within and on him and everybody else was saying that he needed to go and his disciples needed to go and bring **this good news** (this gospel) **about this kingdom's power** in us to others also, which they did. They needed to explain "Gods" ways of doing things in his kingdom to everybody. Miracles started to happen to demonstrate this powerful energy of this kingdom (quantum energy field) to anybody who wanted to listen.

The kingdom of "God's" power and essence (energy) is within us and everybody else, and we are capable of far more than we can imagine. We are all anointed (covered and filled with this yoke destroying energy power) because "God" shows no partiality and is no respecter of persons. In Acts 10:34 Peter opened his mouth and said: "In truth I perceived that God shows no partiality." We have seen that every person is as important and is the same as any other person who ever lived before and after Jesus.

That was why Jesus even said that we would do greater works than him with this power or anointing. In John 14:12 Jesus said, "Most assuredly I say to you, he who believes in Me, the works that I do he will also do, and greater works than these he will do because I go to My Father."

You cannot stop the power from working, but you can control it yourself if you know it exists and understands how it is working. You cannot do anything to earn this creative power since it is already working within every one of us in all its fullness. The only problem is that not everybody knows about and recognises the existence of this creative energy power within. If power exists and you do not know about it, you will still see its effects everywhere around you, not knowing that you can control it. People often use the explanation that their experience was caused by or due to other people, fate, circumstances, hard work, prayers, Buddha, Jesus, the devil, faith, fasting, curses, a guardian angel, etc, but in the end, we now know that it all comes from this creative power inside ourselves that we now rediscover. You are not what happened to you, you are whom you choose to become, so you need to do it deliberately. You need to use these powerful scientific truths intentionally, otherwise life is not going to work exactly the way you want it to work.

This powerful energy of the kingdom of "God" is inside us. In Luke 17:21 Jesus Christ said, "Neither shall they say Lo here or lo there for behold the kingdom of God is within us." In us means in absolutely everybody. In any kingdom there are laws and ways of doing things and it is the same in this kingdom (energy field), there is a way of doing things. At the core of everything, this is the only kingdom or energy field that has ever existed and will ever exist.

If this kingdom of God is in you, who are you then? You first need to seek this kingdom in you and its ways of doing things, then all things will be added unto you. You just need to see and choose to control it and not be controlled by it.

The kingdom of God (the quantum energy field in consciousness) and its powerful ways of doing things are still supposed to be the main message (the good news) we are to bring to everybody on earth seeing that that was also the main message, the good news that Jesus preached and asked his followers to do, and we also still need to do. We are not to think of this creative energy power in any other way. As we now have seen, these doctrines of Jesus were appropriate and should be implemented consciously.

We all need to find out exactly how this creative kingdom power in the universe is working otherwise our happiness and abundance will be built on the wrong foundation, out of the ego-mind (the false sense of self) and will not last.

The good news is that you do not need direction or help from any religious teacher, pastor, guru, mystic, or saint on finding this power and on how to live life. You need to go within as already proven where this power and knowledge already exists, and then you just need to listen to and trust your higher inner being using your feeling for guidance on how to use this power wisely to live a happy, free, and fulfilled life.

If we only follow our current beliefs from our parents, teachers, and society and not from the guidance within, we are limited to what is already created, and nothing new and fresh can happen in our life. Our higher true nature will lead us to all knowledge when we connect through our awareness to this kingdom where we live in this reality inside ourselves.

In 1 John 2:27 we read, "**But the anointing which ye have received of him abides in you and ye need not anyone teach you** but as the same anointing teaches you all things, and is truth, and is no lie, and even as it hath taught you ye shall abide in him." As seen before, all the knowledge and power in the world is inside us, so we just need to connect and listen to our higher inner true self. Our higher inner self (the energy field within) will lead us, and we need to and can only trust it for our path. So, we really are only allowed to follow our higher self for the direction of any of our desires. Rumi said, "Everything in the universe is within you, ask all from yourself." Our children and we need to just always follow the guidance, the feelings from within and not from anybody else.

You are not ordinary or broken and need to become extraordinary. You also do not need to or must change; you just need to realise and be who you already really are. You are not whom you were told you are, you are a kind divine being with divine power and intelligence from within. You are powerful and extraordinary already and just need to realise this and be who you really are. Your old beliefs and understanding of who you are where wrong and are holding you back. You are worthy of everything you desire and need to love yourself unconditionally. We are all meant to shine.

This was the good news that Jesus wanted to make available to every human being on earth. Every one of us is responsible for our own salvation on earth, meaning we need to take charge of our own freedom. The more we use this creative powerful energy, the more we will trust this powerful energy within, causing deliverance and abundance in all areas of our life.

The power has been and is always working but can only be available to be used by those who know how to use it. We need to repent, change our thinking, and start living in this creative power of this rediscovered kingdom realm. We will discuss this powerful kingdom in the next chapter. In Mathew 16:16 we read, "And Simon Peter answered and said, thou art the Christ the Son of the living God."

Simon Peter is acknowledging that Jesus was filled with this powerful energy of "God" and is the son of "God", and as you have seen, we all have been filled (anointed) and are all also sons of "God" with all its privileges and powers.

If you believe you are just a person (a human with a mind and body), you believe in separation which is just an appearance. There is no other being but this godly energy field. We do have separation just as a temporary experience, but the truth is we eternally are one, and there is no duality or separation in this non-dual universe at all. You can never be and have never been separated from this godly energy field, you can only believe you are separated or be unaware you are not separated or even refuse to accept that you are not separated. This divine creative powerful energy is in everything and everybody, including in Jesus and you.

These revelations and truths make us no different from Jesus or anybody else that ever lived, lives or will ever live.

All mystics like Jesus, which we find in every main religion are people who realise this union, this oneness with "God" or the quantum energy field. If you accept that you are part of this energy field, it means that you can also be in control of your own destiny, just like Jesus.

We now know scientifically that everyone on earth is filled with this same creative power, but not everybody realises or knows about its existence. In fact, we cannot exist without this divine powerful energy source or quantum energy field within us. It is not exclusive to only a chosen few as some people wanted to proclaim in the past but is for anyone to be used who wants to hear and understand that it does exist.

PAUL'S KINGDOMS POWER / CHRIST IN US

In the New Testament we find the word christ being defined as somebody who is filled (anointed) with the power of "God." The word christ means the "anointed one and his anointing," or one who is anointed (filled and smeared) with the essence (power, energy) of "God." Christ is the powerful higher self. Paul said it was the risen or resurrected christ in us, our powerful higher self in us that was important. Christ, our higher self with the power of "God" needs to be awakened and be resurrected in us as it was dead in us in our ego-mind.

We need to awake and resurrect the knowledge of the risen christ in us. We need to recognise and get the complete revelation of what the risen awakened christ in us (our higher self) means. This powerful energy source, christ within us will need to wake up, rise up, be resurrected in us from the dead, and then the resurrected christ in us can be alive as the power source in us again. Only to realise and know this, can this christlike power be in us in all its fullness.

Paul said that he received a vision of the resurrected or risen christ (our higher self) in us who commissioned him to preach this good news of the kingdom to the gentiles (non-Jews). The Bible is often talks about christ in you, the hope of glory, meaning this christlike creative energy power of the kingdom is in you in all its fullness.

In Cor 1:27 Paul said, *"which is christ (this divine energy, spiritual power, anointing) within and among you the hope of glory."* Know that christ is in all, as all, and lives through all. In Cor 2:4 Paul said, "And my speech and my preaching was not with enticing words of man's wisdom but in the demonstration of Spirit and of power (as the risen christ in you)." Just like Paul and Jesus Christ, you have a huge potential and creative power available for you to use.

Paul, who was from Tarsus and understood Philo spoke more of the Greek mind. He did not talk about Jesus Christ's trial, crucifixion, resurrection and what he taught as a religion but about how he viewed *christ within as an eternal unseen powerful source.* This christ in us needs to be first recognised, then crucified (the ego-self whom we think we are needs to die) and then the realisation of the higher inner self and its power needs to be resurrected or rise up in us.

Paul suggested that the second coming of Christ (meaning Christ's return) is spiritual and is us waking up to the knowledge of this christ (powerful higher self) within us. Christ in us is the one we were always waiting for to return. It is not Christ returning in the flesh but the realisation of this knowledge of christ consciousness in us, the knowledge of this power in us that is returning

Paul saw and understood Christ as a pre-existing divine eternal energy being that needs to be realised in us. The true second coming is the revelation of our true essential being after it has been stripped from its limitations, christ consciousness in us.

Paul also says in Galatians 2:20, *"And it is no longer I who live but it is christ who lives in me."*

Again, <u>**christ was not Jesus' surname**</u> but the word christ is a recognition of the spiritual creative energy and its power within us. We can also say the *awakened christ within*, the kingdom of "God," which is also the spirit of "God," power of "God," or the power of this energy field within you.

If you say you are a Christian (christ is within), you are confirming that just like Jesus Christ, you realise that you have this christ power within and are filled with this same christlike powerful creative energy. All christians at the time of Jesus understood this powerful energy within and that was why they were called christians (christ is within). As we can now see, *we are all christians, having this christlike power within, but not everybody has got this revelation knowledge. The christ (powerful higher self within) must rise up from dead in you and become awakened, alive, and be recognisable* as it was with Jesus. You need to become christ conscious. You need to crucify your ego-mind (false sense of self) and then let the power of God (your higher self, the risen christ, consciousness) be awakened, be resurrected, or rise up from within you. The word christ again means the anointed (you) and the anointing (your powerful energy). Christ within you then means you are filled with burden removing, yoke destroying powerful energy to live a happy and abundant life.

As we understand quantum physics now, it is explaining that the exact same creative power that is the essence of everything is in all of us, we just need to recognise it. *"God' has ordained no individual one. This power is for every one of us to be used for salvation, to live in abundance.*

This means we are all christs, e.g., Patricia Christ, Anne Christ, or Jacob Christ, but we are not Jesus Christ.

We need to recognise the complete revelation of what the risen christ and his power within us means and this knowledge needs to become real and can be used by all of us. *This knowledge was and still is the mystery knowledge known by prophets, mystics, and sages throughout the ages. Remember, it is not by faith in what Jesus Christ did but of what he told us who we really are and this christlike power in all of us.* Jesus Christ cannot be in you, only christ, this powerful creative energy can be in you. *You now need to see christs power in everything.*

Again, we see in John 14:20 Jesus said, "... you will know absolutely that *I am in my Father, and you are in me, and I am in you."* When Jesus said that the father and I are one, he meant that we all are one since we all are from the same essence and likeness of "God." What I essentially am and what "God" essentially is, is one and the same energy in consciousness. "God" is not an all-powerful being outside you.

At our highest level, we are all gods, and this is not blasphemy but our actual identity, Jesus said so. In John 10:34 Jesus replied, *"Is it not written in your law, I have said you are gods",* and Psalm 82:6 says, *"You are gods, you are all sons of the Most High."* Jesus was "God" in the flesh, and so are you. We are all together "God" and "God" is all together us. "God," Jesus is in or part of consciousness in the same measure as we are in or part of consciousness. This also then means that *any thought* about a personal God is and cannot be God. Consciousness is the essence of who we all are, even after death. We are consciousness, we are the creator, and we are "God," we are all gods.

If you do want to use the word "God," that is okay as long as you remember that this essence of consciousness is all oneness and contains everything including "God," Jesus, me, and you and everything else in all its fullness.

As we know by now, we are all extensions of the energy field and we deliberately decided to descend here as Jesus did. There is no "God" up there that is going to come and help you. *Just like Jesus, you decided yourself to descend into this density or realm to come experience and manifest whatever you desire.*

Jesus Christ was holy and divine, and from the quantum energy field, and so are you. He was no more special than you, and you do not need him in order to be more divine. Gen 1:27 reads, "So God created man in his own image." You really need to turn to the real source of everything namely consciousness, the quantum energy field within. Your devotion cannot be in the opposite direction to the source energy from which it arises, so you need to get rid of the dualistic image, object, or persona you are devoted to because you are the "I am that I am."

You and only you can know your real feelings to which the universe will react.

Yes, you do not need any advice or guidance from any self-help book, spiritual person, saint, or guru, because you have living guidance within you that will and is responding to every thought you are thinking. In 1 John 2:27 we read. ***"But the anointing which you have received from Him remains in you, and you do not need anyone to teach you. For as the same anointing teaches you concerning all things and is truth, and is no lie, and even as it has taught you, remain in Him."*** You need to listen to your higher inner self only for any advice.

Nobody else except you can be your teacher to live your life because other people cannot connect to your higher eternal self (awareness, consciousness) for all your truths, feelings, and desires. Mathew 23:10 said, "Nor are you to be called teacher for you have got one teacher, the Christ," saying that you only have one teacher who is christ (your higher inner self, the creative power) in you, not any pastor, priest, or guru.

Do not listen to anybody else about what is possible and necessary for you. You are the creator and are responsible to navigating your own life. You only need to follow the guidance from your eternal higher inner self. Guidance for successful living is always from christ, the power within. I also believe that this is the way we need to teach our children to live, listen and walk according to their eternal inner self (creative energy or christ power within).

Manifesting our desires is not about attracting what you want but is an awareness and understanding that you attract who and what you are, your state of being. Yes, to be different, we need to go beyond our minds and go into being who we really are. We need to do things because it is who we really are, and we need to *be* just that in our thoughts, feelings, and acts. **The better we know ourselves, the less we will fear but trust our own power.** We are all just part of this one creator and creation. We need to *be who we really are*. So, we need to think, feel, and act accordingly, and everything will change and manifest to our benefit. John 10:34 also states that you are entirely part of the creative energy field of "God."

As said before, we do not want to know what you have or where you have been, but only want to know who and what you really are as a very powerful eternal energy being. Judging oneself to be inferior to others is one of the worst acts of pride because it is the most destructive way of being different.

You do not understand these truths if you think you are different from anybody and anything else.

The biblical explanation of Jesus' knowledge, truths and his vision are his only gift to you. In the Aramaic Bible in plain English, in John 14:6, Jesus said to him, "I am the living God, The Way and The Truth and The Life; no man comes to my Father but by me." *Jesus was not talking about his body here, and he was also not talking about an afterlife but was talking in the now about our current everyday way of living.* A more accurate explanation of this comment would be that he has the correct knowledge, the truth of who we really are and who "God" really is. We need to come and listen to him, he has the way (accurate knowledge), the truth (facts you can trust) to live life abundantly, and the way to salvation (recovery).

Heaven is right here and right now. There is nowhere else we can go, and when we stop living on earth, we will still completely and eternally exist in the quantum energy field.

This powerful godly spiritual field we are, will continue after death, not our mortal body or our mind. When we as a person die, our awareness withdraws from the physical and thought form and then exists in potential energy as the higher conscious awareness again.

Again, remember that you are an individualisation, a hologram of this energy field, and your body and mind are just a manifestation of it in this world. The biblical explanation of how this creative energy functions in the universe can be explained scientifically by studying quantum science. *You now have the same knowledge, same facts, and same power to live life as Jesus Christ did.*

We are not victims but participants and co-creators and need to choose in which kind of world we want to live. The world is the worst it has ever been, but it is also the best it has ever been. There is no geographical hell or heaven. Hell is just living in a survival mode, and heaven is living in an abundant creative attitude.

Everything in the universe happens by design and is perfect in its seemingly imperfection. Salvation is not for one day in the future. Salvation means to be saved from harm, ruin, or loss, not in a future utopia, but here and now (today) on this planet. Life is supposed to always feel and be good to you.

Paradise, heaven, the kingdom is not coming but it is here and now, we are home already. In fact, we never left. We only left the kingdom because we did not have the knowledge to know it exists. We were always a powerful creative force capable of far more than we have ever imagined, we just did not know it. The kingdom's power always was and is available in the here and now for anybody who wants to listen and understand this re-established and newly discovered knowledge.

TRUTH, TRUST, AND FAITH, WHAT IS RIGHT?
Trusting truth is the most intelligent act in existence because truth is the basis on which life operates and creates. We need to trust one hundred percent that we can manifest our desires. *The difference between truth and blind faith is therefore of the uttermost importance to manifest your desires with abundance.* Before we can continue and live a successful life, we really need to grasp these truths

properly because what we accept to believe or trust as true, is true or will become true for us.

We know that the quantum energy field is an informative energy field and if we ask, we will get an answer every time. We cannot blindly accept the faith and truths of other people anymore. We need to question everything and come to our own conclusions about what is true or what is not. This is not blasphemy but courage and the right thing to do. (We rather do blaspheme when we say we are separated and not part or one with "God" (the energy field). A truth is not created but only discovered.

Only a truth and the discovering and experiencing of a truth will heal our body and mind and make us whole, whereas any belief system will block our development.

You do not have to have blind faith in truth for it to operate. *Truth is working whether you believe it or not because it is factual knowledge, it is science.*

The most important requirement to manifesting anything is your trust that it will happen. When you trust, you let things happen itself and it will. You can trust that if you put this new knowledge into action whether it is true science and not just a hope that something will happen. Truth always feels good and gives you a non-resistant abundant feeling. The only good is knowledge, and if you really want the truth, you will question what I am questioning, and I am sure you will come to the same conclusion.

What you trust is what will become true every time.

John 8:32 says, "And you shall know (understand) the truth and the truth (your understanding) shall make you free." There will be a feeling of absence of any resistance.

Believe means your ignorance has been covered. *Faith is often to believe in the absence of any evidence, and this then is a mistake, we rather believe when we have got evidence.* Faith or belief is formed in your subconscious mind when you surrender to a thought (right or wrong) and keep thinking the thought repetitively until it is hardwired in your subconscious mind. A belief, e.g., religious faith is not a truth, it is only what you believe to be true or accurate, and that can change.

Belief or blind faith is also the ability to surrender to uncertainty and step into the unknown which would be wrong. Belief or faith causes doubt and a feeling of resistance because if you do not give your mind proof, it will not entirely believe. **You blindly believe because you have doubt.** Therefore, belief is an antidote to doubt, and it is necessary to cover doubt. Blind faith or belief is often just a leap in the dark. All blind faith e.g., religious belief, is based on past experiences and is just an opinion, and everybody can have whatever opinion they want; however, we do not need to believe it. Blind faith or belief is the opposite to trust. Most of our blind faith or belief comes from outside, what we are told, opinions from other people, history, science, family, religion, culture, friends and what we therefore faithfully blindly believe. **Faith is often just trusting lousy evidence.** Don Miguel Ruiz Jr said, "The truth does not need us to exist, but a belief does, and sometimes we confuse the two." Truth never needs to defend itself; it is perfect and complete. It is not created but only discovered.

Remember that someone else will always take control of our minds if we do not have our own truths.

Faith then is to believe in something often without evidence or proof, and we are blinded without evidence. (It is like driving with your eyes closed). Therefore, every single person can have a different faith and it does not matter because it is not necessary based on truth.

Truth is based on certainty and not on blind faith or belief. Trust is where you do not have doubt. Generally, people use blind faith to try to get rid of negative or contradictory thoughts (doubt). Because of blind faith, I do not like to use the word faith or belief

because it is difficult to distinguish between true faith and blind faith. **I prefer to use the word trust**.

You are worthy of creating whatever you desire; if you trust a truth, your desires will realise every time.

A positive manifestation can never happen if there is any doubt in your thinking process. Remember, doubt disables any faith and therefore blocks any creation. What you doubt will be created which often happens with faith. Faith is blind and only works for simple-minded people e.g., a child. It will never work for thinking people because they always entertain negative or contradictive doubtful thoughts, e.g., too difficult, not possible, not sure, hope, etc. **Any doubt causes an incomplete faith.** When you become a thinking person, your faith is not too deep because somewhere doubt (distrust) will always crop up, which will cancel your faith and disables your manifesting.

You need to trust the truth, which will not cause any doubt.

That is why you cannot be sincere while praising and worshipping somebody you do not fully trust. You cannot use blind faith in trusting somebody you do not trust. It will lead to a performance attitude, which will lead to doubt and disabling manifestation again.

The truth is we only consist of energy, so all the creative power in us is us. We have the creative power to change our desires and destiny. Self-trust will predict whether you will create exactly what you desire. Trust yourself that you are the energy field and an extension of the energy field and not a puppet being controlled by anybody on your outside. Self-trust means you confidently rely on your wholeness, including your character, ability, strength, and your truth. **To be unsure of your true identity will create distrust and will block any desired manifesting.** This is heaven right here, we are in it right now, and we do not need to adopt any belief system. We only need to live according to these rediscovered essential truths. Do you want the knowledge of the truth and trust or just believe the unknown and doubt? Your heart always needs to be devoted to this truth.

THE SPIRITUAL AND HUMAN MIND:
All of us are one hundred percent human and one hundred percent spiritual just like Jesus, Buddha, mystics, sages, and any person that ever lived. Humans inside the created universe consisting of energy are operating in this world with their human nature (finite earthly mind) and their spiritual nature (infinite spiritual mind). Our higher

spiritual self is totally integrated with our lower atomic self as a specific energy pattern. So, there is no real distinction between the spiritual and material self. Our human part is just an imaginary limitation of our spiritual part, so our human mind is just a limitation of the spiritual mind. A finite mind is needed to have an objective experience.

The spiritual mind (higher inner self) limits itself, and this limitation of itself is needed so that the human experience can be fully human and can fully be lived as a human being (The mystics are using the concept of loss of memory to explain this needed limitation.)

The spiritual mind (energy field), although limiting itself, still has all the qualities of a human being and can fully relate to and experience itself as a human being. As the spiritual mind has all the same qualities as a human mind it can therefore experience to be joyful, happy, peaceful, compassionate, grieving and suffering etc., just like us, with us and as us.

So, the spiritual mind (energy field) is fully aware of the human mind through which it experiences the world. However, the human mind is only partially in relationship with the spiritual mind (quantum energy field). Although the spiritual mind limits itself, it still continuously relates to us, and we can have a relationship with it and also use its power to create abundance on earth.

For the energy field (consciousness) to create a world with beings to exist that do evolve over time it needs to be perfect and imperfect simultaneously.

That means that the energy field (spiritual mind, our higher inner self) is continuously in the process of changing and expanding in this created universe. When we leave this story, we lose our body and mind and become hundred present spiritual energy again.

All emotions, feelings, and thoughts (The ego-mind) are part and a creation of consciousness. No experience is harmful, and fear is also not bad. **If you are suffering, you are just holding on to something that is not the truth.** It is all a teaching and a blessing, but the blessing only comes when we learn the lesson intended by the experience.

Nothing is separate from this quantum energy field meaning this field is manifesting, allowing and is responsible for good and evil to exist and to play a role in earth's evolution process. Opposites appear in this divine duality, but it is just an appearance, there is no good, bad, right, or wrong, they are all harmonising. We need to understand that evil is not the opposite of good, but the lack of it, meaning evil is not to be resisted or fought against but to be accepted as it is, and needs be replaced with good. That then also means no separate dualistic devil needs to be conquered.

Heaven is everything that appears and arises around you. The universe is using your eyes to observe his creations. Everything is beautiful and perfect; you just need to take time to discover and find the beauty in everything. At the core of everything, all is one, and there is no image or object but only the divine conscious field expressing itself in different ways. As mentioned before, the current acceptable consensuses are that consciousness is the fundamental source of everything.

If you see this conscious energy field as "God," remember that God the Son and the Holy Spirit are also part of this one godly conscious energy field and there is no need for any object idolatry. There is no separate dualistic "God" as an image or object we need to submit to, exalt or worship.

In John 10:34, Jesus replied, **"Is it not written in your law, I have said you are gods",** and Psalm 82:6 says, **"You are gods, you are all sons of the Most High."**

We need to expand the view we have of ourselves. No goal will get us where we already are. If we say we are sons of "God," all it means is that we are extensions or manifestations of this unseen godlike energy field. I do see myself as part of this godly divine energy field in consciousness that some people call "God" and of which I have exactly the same essence, nature, and likeness. We just need to be the divine and holy beings that we already are. We are already whole, beautiful, and kind. Again, we are far more than the physical body we live in and only need to have memory loss to fully live as a mind and body.

We are an extension and manifestation of a complicated quantum entangled energy field that is responding to our emotions and thoughts to produce and create the world we want to live in. This all means that the universe then exists because we are creating it and creating it as we go, it is continuously evolving and expanding. *The perfection of who we and the universe are, constantly expanding through all our manifestations.*

You already are an infinite eternal being with no beginning and no end, you were never born and will never die. Due to the creating power of your thoughts, your body changes the whole time, but at your core (your aware being), you never change and stay the same forever.

You are not a victim; you can now manifest your own reality, and there is nothing you should ever deprive yourself of. With your thinking, anything can get bigger or smaller. You can have whatever you desire, but you need to make choices in line with who you really are.

Abundance in all areas of your life starts in your mind with an abundant feeling. How you think and how you feel creates your new being, meaning you can improve your state of being any time you wish. You will have and will become exactly what you think about. Henry Ford said, "Whether you think you can or you think you cannot, you are right" because what you feel and expect is the vibrational frequency you radiate into the universe and then will attract and make active in your experience.

You are enlightened now, which means that you have come to the end of your seeking and having this self-knowledge back again will bring you lasting inner peace. You are healed now, which means your memory of your holiness and wholeness exist in its fulness again. You are all-knowing, all-powerful, and unlimited. You do not need any more teachings or teachers to tell you who you are and what you can and must do.

You are an eternal infinite spiritual formless being having a temporal human experience, and this is by far the most important truth and foundation to live by.

The accumulation of material wealth is not the source of your joy and happiness. If you do know who you truly are, you will love yourself and will forever be happy. You were born with kindness, peace, joy, and happiness inside you, so peace, joy and happiness, and kindness are your true nature, just be that. ***The knowledge of who you are, your true identity is really all that matters.*** Everything else will fall into place after you have realised this truth.

Never ever doubt who you really are. You are not a victim of this world; you are the world. You are not broken, and you do not need to fix anything about your past, yourself, your emotions, or anything else. You know a great deal more than you think you know. You can now also see that you do not need any psychotherapy or any motivation of any kind or from anybody, ***you just need to know and be who you already are.*** You just need to be comfortable with your true identity, who you truly are and always have been. Many of your beliefs about yourselves are just beliefs, and you take them as the absolute truth without questioning them which is wrong. Existence knows no past or future, only now. You can now see that there is no geographical heaven or hell where you can go to when you die, eternity is here and now and will always only be here and now. Even your biological death is just an appearance and are just based on a false premise.

You are beautiful, kind, perfect, whole, successful, and complete and an extension and one with a godly energy field, holy and divine, and a son of "God" just like Jesus was with all its privileges and powers to be used. I am "God" is not blasphemed; it is our true identity. You are magnificent and eternal and already possess infinite wisdom and infinite potential from within you; you just need to be yourself.

You are the creator that created you, and you can never separate yourself from this source energy that is you. There are no shortages in this universe, and you came here to create or manifest your own reality and abundances in harmony and unity with your higher infinite true self. Just relax, be aware of yourself and be who you really are as a spiritual energy being having a human experience. You are a unique timeless being, and you can choose to participate in the way you want this reality to unfold. ***You also now realise that you can have as many***

lives as you want. Peace and happiness cannot leave you, and you will never die. You have nothing to do but just enjoy your unique self and let be what will be. An effort is really the practising of resistance that blocks your creation.

You need to realise to be your true identity first before you start each day. If you are convinced of how extraordinary, unique, and special you are, everything will change for good. You are not just a human! You are powerful beyond measure. You are a super-human being who only dreams that he is just a limited human being.

The real you are not the person you see in the mirror. You must consciously and continuously remind yourself of the truth of who you really are. Knowing your true identity will help you effortlessly to be your higher eternal you.

You are a son of "God," and you are already free from all human limitations, there is no reason to worry about anything. It is this self-knowledge of your beingness, of who you truly are and not what you are doing or having that brings enjoyment and happiness in your life.

The nature of eternal beings is that there will always be something new you desire and thereby causing the universe to grow and expand. You are an abundant being and can now plan and create your own future by using your imagination to build an image in your mind of how you desire to experience yourself in life, and it will be so.

A genuine desire will always be an honest desire. A genuine desire will always feel great, and you will honestly want it in your life without any agenda or contradictory thoughts from your ego-mind. ***A genuine desire will be the ideal next step for you to accomplish.*** A genuine desire will be what your eternal higher-self desire. If you genuinely know who you are, you will know that whatever you desire to do (usually your first thoughts) is what consciousness, your true higher self, also desires to do. Know that the higher self does not ever think about small-scale things.

I do want to emphasize that you cannot improve yourself by reading self-help books or listening to a preacher because ***they are only***

talking to your mind, which you cannot really control. The only way to make or improve yourself is to find out about what truth is, and that is discovering who you really are; then you will become to be of sound mind.

In the next chapter, with the fact that we are the created and the creator of our own story will discuss the process of how our imagination (our focused thoughts and feelings) will manifest our personal reality. We do need to live from our divine self from now onwards.

CHAPTER 3

SELF-MASTERY: HOW TO LIVE DIVINELY AND MANIFEST ABUNDANCE IN THE QUANTUM FIELD

We now know that our whole life is just a manifestation, and *we are all creators of our own reality* and can now deliberately participate in the way this reality unfolds. We need to regulate and take full responsibility for our own life now. In the past, to change our future, we waited for our circumstances or an experience from the outside to change our senses, which changes our thoughts and emotions, and then feelings, leading to a manifestation.

There is now a new understanding of the true nature of our reality which is saying that by being aware or conscious, we participate in a mind-made world and are in control of our own ultimate destiny. *The universe does not use words to speak, only frequency. We now know that feelings are the non-verbal language, the frequency which we use to speak and attract our desired reality from the energy field.* With this new model as now seen, we can change our conscious feelings by changing our thoughts and emotions deliberately from the inside, which will then manifest to change our future reality.

We are eternal beings, and this means we will always have desires, asking for more. This is the way the universe is established and causes it to expand. We are creating new desires as we go, and this will never stop. Desire is the need to add something to yourself in order to have the feeling of having it and be yourself more fully. When you manifest, you just manifest another aspect of yourself. *Whatever you desire already exists.* We do need to control our desires and always need to distinguish between a personal desire which will not bring any fulfilment and an impersonal desire that comes from our true eternal self, that will be in line with what the universe desire to expand; it arises on behalf of the whole.

Science has done away with the old fundamental Newtonian principle of cause and effect. *Quantum physics, the physics of possibility now explains all our old spiritual principles of the past much clearer.* This new better model which we call the quantum model explains that *your mind manifests* your reality where when you think (having an intention) and have an emotion, a feeling occurs that attract a specific experience in your reality. *Our life will be a mirrored image of our thoughts (mind).*

We do now know the electromagnetic field manifests matter, and if you change the field, you manifest matter. We change the field with our thoughts and feelings. This means we must manifest from the electromagnetic field instead of from matter. We cannot see this energy field, but we can feel it, and *what we think, and feel will turn into our reality as real stuff and experiences.* This also shows that our thoughts are more powerful than our actions, and hard work will not bring more success.

We now need to use our own mind power before we act. We also now need to define our future deliberately otherwise; we will tend to live in the past and according to the old Newtonian model of cause and effect. We need never to surrender our freedom and allow our outside to control our inside. We are not ever allowed to surrender our free will to our circumstances or our environment. We either create our own reality, or our own reality is being controlled by our outside environment, and so, it will be created for us.

We possess an untapped potential within us and are here to enjoy and live a happy and fulfilled life. Life then is not supposed to be a competition at all because we can all have the life we desire and deserve. We were born rich, and abundance in all areas of our life is our birthright. *The same power that made us will also heal and save us.* This is a vibrational universe, and we are a field of energy where our thoughts do the asking and allowing. Our thoughts radiate a cosmic vibration frequency wave-like a broadcasting tower into the universe that penetrates all time and space. We are always offering a vibration of what we are thinking about. We have the ability to choose our own thoughts. We have got complete control over our vibration but usually do not exercise it. The way we want to experience life is now in our hands with this powerful energy field available to manifest all our desired experiences which all already exist, and all already belong to us.

We are not victims of our outer world anymore and wherever we are now is irrelevant. Only where we are going is important and where everything is. We are powerful creators that create our own purpose and our own reality from within. We become what we think about, and our external reality then reflects who and what we think are true of ourselves internally (our self-concept or personality). If we change our inner world (personality), which we always can, our outer world will change. *So, we need to change our personality (our self-image or self-concept), which includes our thoughts, feelings, and acts, to change our personal experiences.*

The universe is an energy field of consciousness awareness full of information and possibilities, and we are extensions of it. Consciousness can take on any form and be any kind of matter. We need to stop looking at particles (seen matter on the outside) to manifest our desires through cause and effect and start to use the quantum energy field model (unseen energy field within and around us) through thoughts and emotions for manifestation of our reality. *This quantum energy view tells us now that there is a wave, particle*

duality meaning matter can behave as a particle and a wave and an observer can affect and collapse the waveform, forming a particle. Energy can be explained as a force that has the capacity to do work and the influence to cause an action.

As we know by now, we are all an extension and an integral part of this one energy field in consciousness.

There is no empty space, only energy and nothing else. Everything is energy moving at different frequencies of vibration. What we desire already exists in the energy field meaning we are not separate from what we desire. We are one with everything we want but just cannot see it because of the different energetic vibrational frequencies it is in before it manifests.

Everybody and everything are part of this energy vibrating at infinite different frequency levels, and there is nothing else in existence. As we also know by now is that every different thought frequency carries and then radiates different information into the quantum energy field. In this quantum energy field, all possibilities exist, and reacting differently to every message received. This then determines how we experience things in life.

If you thought you came here with a purpose, it would have meant then that you would only have been the created and not the creator. However, you are infinite eternal quantum energy having a temporary human experience and a creator creating as you go.

When you demystify quantum physics and understand this science, this truth is not a miracle anymore but becomes an everyday strategy, a method, or a skill. It is still a miracle when we can choose to use the power of our minds to manifest our reality. This knowledge now then means that you are a creator and no longer a victim of your circumstances anymore unless you choose to be one.

As consciousness/awareness, each one of us is a unique infinite creator, and we can have anything we desire. Our desires are natural and never-ending. Life is beautiful and full of technological miracles, and we are part of it and can attract anything we desire; there are no limitations. *We can now prosper without competition wherever we go.*

Again, as you have seen, we are all aware vibrational energy beings that have the ability to choose, direct and navigate the energy with our thoughts. *If your mind then can trust the evidence of who you really are, you will also be able to trust that you can manifest all your desires.* You are always busy manifesting, so there is always something you desire that is not yet manifested. Just also remember that suffering is caused by desire, so whatever you desire needs to always come from your true higher self and not from your ego-mind.

As you know by now, all desires already exist in the form of vibrational energy. You are the attractor and creator of all your experiences in life and need to learn how to navigate this energy power yourself. Here we will now discuss the strategy, method, formula, or scientific technique which we can learn to attract and create our own reality.

QUANTUM MANIFESTING - THE NEW WAY:

You do not need to depend on your circumstances to live life but can now navigate your own everyday life purposefully from a field of infinite possibilities. All possibilities exist in the quantum energy field. You have access to this energy field of possibilities and information and draw a certain probability into your reality with a thought and feeling. The non-physical unseen dimension has an infinite supply of everything you desire since all existence is just unlimited energy.

If you are going to do something big and magnificent and unlimited, you need to feel and be magnificent and unlimited. The more you realise your true identity as conscious awareness, the more you will be able to manifest your desires. It is crucial to have a vision of your true identity when manifesting. *Everything depends on your concept of yourself.* What you do not claim is true of yourself, you will never be able to realise. If you know you are powerful, magnificent, and unlimited, it becomes an amazingly simple proses to manifest your own desires.

This is a vibrational universe. *You are all vibrational quantum energy beings, and every feeling and thought (our state of being) causes the energy to vibrate at a specific frequency (level of vibration), broadcasting that specific information pattern into the electromagnetic field into the eternal universe, attracting the same frequency energy from the field of infinite possibilities, then causing an experience to happen.* Your choices of your thoughts then matter in your daily reality. *The universe is consistently delivering to you according to your vibration pattern, the version and identity you have of yourself and the version of you as if your desire is fulfilled. This means that how you think and feel creates your state of being.*

The universe does not listen to your words or thoughts but reacts to the vibrational frequency you are radiating from your body as a whole unit consisting of a thought accompanied by a feeling. *This means you need to change your body emotionally before the evidence takes place in your life. You change your body emotionally by having a feeling of gratitude, wholeness, worthiness, and abundance. When you then think a thought that attracts an emotion, you access the creative power of the universe.* The thought waves are cosmic waves and penetrate all space and time, creating an image in the field.

Like energy vibrational frequencies attracts like vibrational frequencies energy causing a manifestation. So, everything you want is on its own energy frequency level, and you need to be in alignment, one with it. Your thoughts and feelings need to operate on the same frequency as the reality you want to be in. As mentioned before, a frequency is the vibration level, and there is an infinite number of frequencies. If you raise your mind to that higher frequency, you will attract everything on that higher frequency.

You need to take time to feel your way into vibrational alignment with your desire and assume you are there.

You need to bring the words (thought, intention, imagination) to life through the power of an emotion that is causing a feeling that radiates and then draws the specific vibrational frequency just like a magnet.

Whatever you are broadcasting out with any feeling, good or bad, will find a vibrational frequency match and will then attract energy back towards you, causing an experience. The moment you feel it, you receive and attract it in vibrational form, just like the corn seed you put in the ground has the full potential to be the stalk of corn. When you manifest, you are not bringing something in from another world, **you only manifest another aspect of yourself from the energy field that is already here.**

The universe does not respond to your words on its own but only to the vibration you are radiating. When the vibrational frequency information pattern agrees with each other, it attracts the same energy, then forming an experience. Your feeling then is an indication of what your vibration and then energy attraction will be. What you feel is what you genuinely expect and will attract into your reality.

You must always give the quantum field something to work with. In the quantum model, you purposefully then need to tell your body emotionally how the future will feel like as if your desired experience happened already before it is going to manifest. **You need to assume the feeling as if it is done.** You now make your future dream a present fact to experience a satisfying feeling. The mind does not know the difference between what you actually experience (the real) and what you feel in your imagination (the unreal). It will manifest if there is not a more powerful feeling in an opposite direction to counteract. As in the past, we are not waiting for some experience on the outside of us to change our emotions or feelings on the inside. We are not using our senses but making a deliberate decision to change our emotions.

Your emotions respond to your thoughts, so you need to just change and refocus your thoughts to change your emotions and then your feelings. You need to become aware of how you want to feel. If you have any specific clear image of an intention with any raised emotion, it will form a feeling, a state of being, a specific frequency that the electromagnetic field around and in your body understands, attracting the desired manifestation or experience. **You need to change the pattern in the field and not the matter itself.** An, e.g., tumour on the body is an appearance of matter, so you need to change the field pattern in your imagination and refocus as if it is done. So, your imagination (thoughts and feelings) then creates your desired reality or event, and the tumour disappears here.

Everything has its own vibrational frequency. Feeling is a conscious awareness of vibration. Listen to your feelings because that is the vibrational frequency you are now in. The vibrational frequency represents the level of conscious awareness we are in. What matters the most is how you feel. *Your best feeling thought, the feeling that speaks the most loudly, will bring you the highest frequency vibration, followed then with the best results.* Your vibration increases or decreases according to the vibration of your thoughts. Remember to always think of thoughts that give you the best feeling; it will cause the highest vibrational frequency.

If your mind and emotions agree on a specific frequency and you stay on that frequency, good or bad, creation will occur. You also do not need to go anywhere to receive, but the experiences you desire get to be drawn like a magnet towards you. In the human heart, the feelings will form electromagnetic waves like radio waves that radiate or emit into an energy field of infinite possibilities attracting a manifestation or experience to you magnetically. What you are feel the most, good, or bad, will come to you.

Set very *clear and specific goals* for what you desire to experience or manifest for you. What you desire is already done on a vibrational level; you just need to come in alignment with it to manifest it. It will then follow after you. It will also come in a way you cannot or must not ever try to predict. If you expect it, it will manifest without effort from your side. Everything will just happen in a natural way. *All your objective reality then is solely produced through your imagination.* We therefore create or participate in our own reality through our thoughts and imagination. The thought then sent the electrically charged signal out, and the feeling draws the experience back to us through the magnetic charge. The picture (thought and feeling) that we see in our mind about what we desire in our future is really a template for trillions of atoms to organise as a manifestation of consciousness.

Thoughts then is the language of our brain and our emotions the language of our body and the feelings in our heart the language of them together, our whole body as one component in unity. The feeling from the heart then do radiates or emanates an electromagnetic message, an energy pattern into the universal field, creating and drawing an equivalent experience back to us.

The driving force that couples the thought forming a feeling is any raised emotion. It is from the heart that the electromagnetic waves extend into the body and eternally into the universal energy field. We do now know that when we are changing the electromagnetic field the atoms in the body are in, we are changing the atoms. The atoms and the electromagnetic field are connected, so if we change one, we change the other.

Again, the quantum energy view tells us now that there is a wave, particle duality meaning matter can behave as a particle and a wave and an observer can affect and collapse the waveform, forming a particle. We do know that every proton in every atom (particle, matter) in our body is constantly and continuously emerging from the energy field and collapsing back into the field rewiring our body and recreating ourselves to the new way that the universe needs to respond to (The Lamb shift). The body then will change with physical evidence to the future experience as if it has already occurred. Your body now lives in a new world, and due to quantum entanglement, this new information emits into eternity, and the universe then needs to and will change us and our experiences to the new picture or vision of our feelings and images in our mind. This means that if you focus on an alternative perception of yourself, you literally become the person of your new imagination. The universal energy field then translate the change into the reality of our lives.

The universe then is always delivering to you what your pattern of vibration is, the version of you that you emit. You can only be as abundant as much as you let yourself be. You need to always see yourself in the perfection of your highest vision and version.

We then are just distortions of this electromagnetic field constantly collapsing in and re-emerging out of this energy field into whatever template we have formed of ourselves.

Our reality is based upon the vibration that comes from our being. This means that **our personal reality is a reflection or mirror image of our personality**, meaning whom we think and trust we are. **This means that if we want to change our personal reality, we need to change our personality.** We have no fixed personality. **We change our personality by changing our thinking, feeling, and acting.** We really are powerful beings in disguise and can grow in a new version with a new vision of ourselves whenever we desire to. We change the world around us by what is happening inside us with our thinking, feeling and acting.

Our thoughts hold unlimited creative power. We have to become in our thoughts what we try to be and manifest, and the universal energy field will match the vibration and will react accordingly. True manifestation is when we are intentionally becoming the next great version of ourselves. This is how we change our personal life and reality and also why we possess within us all the accomplishing power to manifest all our desires.

You need to realise you are already whole and have got all the creative power you need to achieve all your desires. Change your personality and choose to feel whole, joyful, happy, free, and fulfilled and be that person, and it will then draw the same reality and circumstances towards you into your reality. This then also means that the more you feel whole, the less you will live in lack.

Before manifestation, you need to deliberately withdraw your mind from where you are and then concentrate on having a specific clear thought (intention, imagination) of who you are and what you desire. You then need to choose to feel the success as if your desire is fulfilled. You need to choose to feel the feeling and give thanks that your desire has already been answered and is already real to you. **Only when you can feel it, can you see it, and you can choose the way you feel at any time.**

The universe will bring you precisely the same experience as the feeling you are having. This means you need to teach your body emotionally how to feel, and it really must be a knowing feeling. This means that for your manifestation to happen, you need to know you feel whole before your healed, you need to know you feel successful before you will be successful, you need to know you feel abundance before you will generate wealth, and you need to know you feel loved before you can be loved, you need to know you feel empowered before your success, etc, etc. The opposite of all these feelings is also true e.g., if you live by a feeling of lack, you will create more lack. As mentioned before, there are infinite different thought-feelings, so wherever you are, always reach for your best feeling thought you can find. In the past, we did not realise the importance of our feelings and were brought up to suppress our emotions and feelings, including our gut feelings. We do now understand that directed emotions with pure feelings are everything in creating abundance, and we can control that.

ALWAYS KEEP FOCUS / ATTENTION:

We manifest exactly what we put and keep our minds focused on. We must keep and stay on the vibration of our desire. That which we feel ourselves to be, we are. Our persistent focus keeps the momentum and then brings our specific desire into our life. To attract, we need to be in harmony and maintain the same focused feeling of our desire because whatever we persist in keeping focus on, we give more energy. *If you have a focused feeling on anything, it has already happened and is already coming to you. By keeping our focus and attention on a thought, we maintain the modified feeling state of our body and keep the vibrational frequency of the vision that is radiated consistent.* We need then to control our focus because whatever we give the most focus and significance on is what we will manifest, even if we do not want it. We are all divine creators and can deliberately choose and attract our own desires towards us with our feelings (unity of a thought and emotion). Our focus controls our thoughts, and our persistent focus is creating our reality. Our expectations must be in line with our desires. It will be easier to keep our focus if we are passionate about our desire. We need to make our desire more real than our outside world. We need to passionately keep our focused feeling the entire time about the direction of our desires. This will then radiate the same needed consistent vibrational frequency (information) into the universe.

We control the end result we want to create by maintaining a clear focused picture and pure feeling of the wanted experience. This then also means that whatever we really think and expect is going to happen, is going to happen because we are offering a focused feeling and persistent steady vibration of that what we think. ***We need to take care of how we think and feel more than anything else because any changed feeling will change our destiny.***

It is only our own personal habitual focus then that is important in our creation, and again, we do not need help from anybody else. The opposite then is also true; if we do take our focus away from thoughts and things we do not want, it no longer exists as a vibrational factor in causing an attraction of an experience.

If you do not want something in your life, just deactivate or disable it by changing your focus to something else that is more positive. All the feeling-thoughts we ever thought are still in existence, and they are just not empowered or focused on and therefore in an inactivated state.

Our mind (inner world) and its thoughts then do not just change our physical body but also our physical reality around us (our outer world). Epigenetics proves that our mind is in absolute control of our biology, as proven by ***the placebo and nocebo studies.*** According to Greg Braden, it has been scientifically tested and proven that our emotions change the DNA in our body and that the DNA in our body changes protons (matter) around us. ***Thus, our emotions influence matter.*** We need to create from the electromagnetic field instead of from matter, and by changing the field, we change the matter. By controlling and changing your feelings, and your mood, you change the field in your body and rewrite your own body's chemistry which is changing you physically and mentally. Although your feelings influence matter, you are not really created it, but you instead manifested it by you rearranging reality and then attracting the desired experience into your life.

THIS PRESENT NOW MOMENT:

Your entire life is always in the now moment. **Only this present eternal now moment exists, it is all there is and ever will be, and we are all one with it.** There is no time lapse in the deep inner self, meaning everything is already here, everything is in the timeless now. **All our creative power is also only available in this now moment. Only your feelings then that are in the now can and will manifest.** Everything you are looking for; all possibilities exist in this present now moment in the eternal quantum energy field as energy and as a potential possibility. In our reality, the future and past do not exist. All experiences are in the now. To live life, this present eternal now moment is really all there is and where we always need to be.

We can only manifest in the now by affirming it and see it in the now. Our feelings and trust of any desire to manifest must be a feeling experience as if it is in now in our life already. In future, we will also just live life in the now because this present now moment will not exist anymore.

We are consciousness using the mind to create and achieve all that what we desire on this planet. All matter and experiences were first a thought form, a focused heartfelt thought. If a thought becomes focused on with enough emotional intensity, it becomes a feeling that has the ability to manifest. You are the master of your own thoughts, and you alone hold the key to every situation in your life to make it as you will. So, the thoughts in your mind have made you who you are. Everything you know about yourself resembles a thought you have had. Everything you are feeling, seeing, hearing, touching, and taste resembles a thought you have manifested. You need to have good thoughts, so you must come out of your current mindset and be truly aware and conscious to change your thinking and reality.

As stated before, whom we think we are, our state of being is what we will attract and accomplish, and as we know, what we think about most of the time we will become. Our outside world will be a mirror of our vision and level of inside vibration. Nothing negative happens to you, it is only because of your vibrational frequency that you attract the experience towards you. You also only have access to the realities with which you synchronised internally, so **you will only manifest to what you are a match to and not what you want.**

HOW TO RAISE YOUR VIBRATION:
You need to increase your vibration if you want a better life for yourselves. The most powerful force to raise your vibration is self-love. The more you know who you really are, your true identity, the more you will have self-love. The more you love yourself, the happier you will be. The happier you are, the more you raise your vibration. When you are in a high vibrational frequency, you become one with your desires, and they will manifest.

Always start your day to find alignment with who you are. You need always to be sure of who you indeed are because you are always increasing your vibration by knowing who and what you really are. The energy vibration level will increase when you consider yourself as worthy to receive. If what you believe of yourself is not in alignment with what you want to create, you will not be able to step into it or sustain your focus on it. A wise man once said, "For as he thinketh in his heart, so is he," meaning, where your mind goes or what you think about will expand, and as you continue to think the same thoughts, so you shall be.

You also must always distinguish between what you feel you should do and what you think you should do.

We need to ask our eternal self in us how to live life in alignment to the way it was intended to be. We are never allowed to take a single action until we align with our wanted emotions and feelings. Always be honest and have sincere thoughts. Do not hold thoughts that are in opposition to your desires. If you change your thoughts and your feelings, you can change your whole future. This means you can change your future with any new clear intention and elevated emotion. Always reach to the thoughts that feel the best and never ever have any contradictory thinking. Remember, the miracle-working power of the universe is within all of us. Hard work is not needed; it is the divine quantum energy field that is causing the growth.

If our feelings align, and if we know our true identity, we will receive all our desires. At the centre of our being we are consciousness/awareness, the creator possessing all the creative power that has ever existed.

This is our universe, and we are not at its mercy, but we are in control of it. We can now create an ideal reality out of our own wholeness. (We can either create our own life or allow it to be created for us.) We can now call all those things that do not exist as if they do. Our natural state is abundance since we are capable and worthy of creating our own reality out of a limitless energy field.

So, when we renew our minds of who we are and then change our wishes and desires accordingly, we will become a new person who will be able to clearly see and understand the functioning of this universal energy field or kingdom. Now we will be able to create and achieve all our own desires of what we want to experience in our reality.

To have a feeling of abundance, you also need to come in complete alignment with the present moment of who you truly are in your essence. You need to change your self-concept, your personality (your thoughts, feelings, and acts) of whom you think you truly are to change your personal reality. (Be careful, your own false self-image can hold you back.)

You need to trust who you are, and realise your true identity, and know that your most dominant thought has manifesting power, then feel what it feels like when your thoughts are answered, then it will manifest. It is crucial to make it happen with the understanding of who we indeed are and the wisdom from this higher true self. Your higher authentic self will also influence you to desire only what is the best for you. You also do need to be confident and assured that your desires are happening now.

POWER OF IMAGINATION / VISUALISATION:

If you want to achieve a big dream then ***visualisation and meditation must be the two most important daily activities in your life.*** The world in which we live is a world of imagination. Everything that exists has once been imagined. ***Visualisation is really the backbone for***

creating what you want, and meditation is an effective way to stay present, which as explained, is also a cornerstone. Your imagination which is yours alone, is the greatest gift with which you can bring any desire from the future or the past into the now moment to be created. ***Visualisation is when you intentionally project a thought.*** You create your reality through your imagination when you imagine it yours as if it already exists. Assume that you already are what you want to be and live-in complete confidence in this assumption.

Although the creation proses is effortless, you still need to take action on your imagination because imagination manifests events. As you do visualisation, the picture goes from your conscious mind into your subconscious mind, and the body begins to believe it is in the future instead of the past, and then will create according to the new picture in your mind. All power for creation is only available in the now, and with imagination, you can bring a desired picture into the now from the future for the subconscious mind to create. You use your imagination to go to the future and bring it into the present moment and live as if it is done, and the brain adapts to that new picture and manifests accordingly.

Remember that the subconscious mind does not know the difference if the picture of the desire to be created it receives is real or what is imagined (unreal), meaning also then that the universe does not regard this reality as more valid than the one you desire to experience.

Neville Goddard, in the early 20th century said, "You must make your future dream or vision a present fact by assuming the ***feeling of your wish fulfilled." You need to believe that you have already received it. You assume that it is yours by imagining you already have got what you want. If a person behaves "as if they", will become that type of person, will produce real physiological changes, which produces real vibrational changes.*** Your subconscious mind accepts what you really trust to be the truth, and once you convince your subconscious mind that you do have what you want, it will proceed immediately to bring it too past.

Thinking then from the end scene, and not just thinking of it, is the beginning of all your miracles. You cannot be or have what you cannot see. You need to imagine and live as if the future has already happened. Visualise ***"as if"*** it came true already. You need to imagine as if you are inside the picture in your imagination. If you do think that things will happen for you in the future, you wrongly affirm that they are not here already. There is a significant difference between ***working towards*** an outcome that is wrong and the idea or thought that it ***already happened.***

You need to put the deliberately chosen desired thought in your mind, and with visualisation, you live your outcome from the end scene in the now, feeling as if it is fulfilled. Whatever you ask will be done. We need to feel relieved that it is here now. This means you need to accept and be satisfied that your manifestation is done and that you already have what you are looking for. ***Remember again, an emotion is not a feeling, so you need to have a feeling of a wish fulfilled and not just an emotion that it is fulfilled.***

Visualisation without a feeling is only in the conscious mind where the focus will not last. Only manifestation from the programmed subconscious mind will happen. Visualising your needs or wants is also wrong and a confession of your lack and of you having no trust.

You need to imagine yourself into the feeling that you already have and also live as if you have it right now while you are busy with your everyday activities. You live as if it is in your life right now, and you are not looking for it. Be in a position as if you have already received and live in it. It must be in your imagination first where you see, touch, and physically moving in that situation, affirming that it exists in the now and not in the future; then you will see it in the material world as a manifestation.

You need to visualise exactly (precisely) what you desire. According to old mystic scriptures, you must also ask without any hidden motives and be surrounded by your answer in this moment, and it will be given. This then is one of the most important activities for manifesting. Through visualisation, you need to put the exact desired picture or image in your mind and need to keep and maintain your focus and attention (a consistent vibration) on it as if it is realised. It needs to feel natural and logical.

You need to use your mind imagining, knowing, accepting, and feeling the joy you would feel having what you desire already. You need to be enveloped by what you desire. The more you imagine it in the now, the more it becomes. So, in the end, you need to imagine yourself in whatever state of being you will be if your wish has been fulfilled. You need to think, feel, be sure and function as if your manifestation is done, and you already have and are busy enjoying it. According to Albert Einstein, imagination is more important than knowledge because knowledge is limited but imagination encircles the world.

Where you go in your imagination is where you will go in real life. You can have what you desire if you first see it carried out in your mind. So, we need to attach a feeling to our imagination while we keep our focused feeling constant as if and until manifestation happens. To impress the subconscious mind with the desirable state, you need to assume the feeling that would be yours had you already realised your wish. No idea can be impressed on the subconscious mind until it is felt. The thought and the feeling then, as stated before changing your state of being, your self-concept and then your experience changes. Feelings then are your prayer and the language you use to speak to your body and to the world. Again, you only receive what you already feel you have.

This all means that you can see something into existence, but you must keep your imagination alive and active.

THE POWER OF GRATITUDE / APPRECIATION:
Gratitude and appreciation are strong emotional signs for the body that it already happened. The more you pay attention to the picture in your mind with gratitude and appreciation, the stronger the emotion and less resistance you will feel.

If you are in a state of gratitude, your body and mind are in the ultimate state of receiving, seeing that in that now moment the body believes it is in the future, *in the present moment, and creates and lives according to this new template or picture.*

Saying and feeling that you are* thankful *are very powerful elements in creating a healthy and abundant you. To receive, you need to be in a state of joyful anticipation. The speed with which these thoughts become things is all about what you are doing in terms of how you think and feel. Gratitude keeps the connection open to the source. The stronger the emotion you feel in your body, the stronger the message you radiate, and the stronger the attraction of your experience will be. In your imagination you go to the end scene and feel or be enveloped by what you desire with focus, worthiness, gratitude, and trust. You need to be thankful that everything will always work out the best for you and is unfolding just the way that it should be. As you also know by now, you already have what you desire to have and already are what you desire to be.

BE BEINGNESS:
We have lost the importance of our feelings and need to reclaim it back*.* ***We only manifest that which is equal to the emotional state we are being in.*** We cannot have what we are unwilling to become and ***be vibrationally***. You do become what you think about. ***How you think and how you feel is your state of being*** and is indicative of what you will draw towards and then happen to you. ***You get what you truly feel whether you want it or not. The universe does not hear your words (thoughts), but only the language of your mood, meaning your feelings is your actual vibrational output, your beingness. The feeling that the image brings to us is more important than the image itself.*** We must take care of how we feel and respond to it appropriately. As said before, you also must feel as if it is already done. So, when in doubt, listen to your feelings to see your future creation and future reality.

THE GESTATION / INCUBATION TIME:
There is also no real timeline for what we want to become a reality, but there is always a gestation period to relapse for things to manifest. What we are looking for is already manifesting as we are looking for it, but there is a law of gestation and incubation, and everything manifests in divine time. Manifesting time is likewise controlled by us being in vibrational alignment to what we desire. ***We will manifest***

when we release any resistant thoughts against the happening of the creation. We must maintain the same vibrational frequency for the specific creation by keeping our focused attention constant during the gestation period for the manifestation to happen. Again, the experience will come to us if we give it our undivided attention. It is only our constant undivided attention and non-resistance that keeps it active. We need to maintain the vibration and ignore reality until we can see the manifestation.

You need to focus without resistance. No effort is allowed from your side. If you can hold the frequency pattern of the feeling, you will manifest it into reality. Remember, you live in an attraction-based realm and do not need to chase after anything. How and when growth will happen is not your business but up to the universe. Hebrews 6:12 even declares, "of them through trust and patience inherit the promises."

We need to detach ourselves from the how and when of the outcome otherwise, we will block or slow the outcome of it. Do not visualise the creative proses. How it will happen is not our problem, we need to leave it to the universe. If we keep querying our creation or waiting for what is supposed to happen, we are in the known again, denying the answer to manifest. It will often happen in ways we cannot possibly imagine and can often surprise us, ***but it will happen in a typical natural manner.***

We are never allowed to question the how or when because that will lead to doubt in our hearts, disabling our manifestation. We are to give our desires a time interval for growth. A farmer does not delve into his planted seeds in the ground to see how they grow because the seeds will surely die. ***Ultimately it will take us as long as it will take us to release our resistance to our desire.***

The traditional Christian belief that "God" is mainly an interventional and personal "God" instead of informative and empowering is wrong. We are the creator with all creative power, and we do decide who and what we want to become. We alone create our own purpose and destiny.

Everybody lives in its own universe, and our thoughts can therefore only affect our own manifestations and not anyone else. Your life is in your hands and there is no one else to change but yourself. You choose your own destiny and level of success and happiness, and whatever you decide will always be the right decision for you for the moment.

Trusting is measurable quantities of energy that we can change precisely to create the effects in *our* lives. The quality of you trusting a truth impacts and also determines how the world reacts and unfolds for you. **This then also means that your trust or belief cannot contradict your desires.**

We then can say that the whole existence is just energy that vibrates in frequencies, and a feeling is just a specific frequency level of a vibration. When we generate a powerful feeling, it will manifest as an experience in our life. By knowing how you are feeling, you know what you are radiating and, therefore will receive. You will get what you think, feel, and expect, whether you want it or not. Take care and invest time considering how you feel. A good feeling thought will manifest into a good feeling manifestation and vice versa.

We were born with the mind of christ (our true higher self) in us, so we always have the power and will be able to think of good thoughts and always manifest the world we want to live in. Because the universe belongs to us and is us, it will always say yes to any of our feelings, meaning we need to and will have to choose the right feelings to get the right manifestations. We are creative powerful beings capable of being, having and doing whatever we want. Your world is really only a reflection of your thinking, and things are always in the process of becoming.

Our thoughts must be organised in such a way that there is no doubt, negativity, insecurity, or resistance about what is possible or not possible.

When we are creating our imagined act, we also need to guard our hearts to what we expose our feelings and emotions to in our daily reality. If we do expose our minds to negative news and negative information, we can produce within us a vibrational frequency that can prevent us from our wanted creation and own wellbeing. It is also not a clever idea to speak to anybody about our desires or creations because that can insecure our trust in the creative process. Jesus, who was profoundly mystical, also never said he would come and do for us that which we cannot do for ourselves. A mystic is one who realises his union with "God." As mentioned before, Jesus's mystic teachings are some of the greatest ever and form the basis for all successful living. Jesus was telling us that there is a new, better, and self-controlled way of living and operating in this world and that we are all worthy to live according to it. We have no reason ever to feel less powerful than him. ***We can only create what we entirely trust is in our power to create. That is why we really need to know without any doubt that we are consciousness, which is our true identity, otherwise we will not be able to fully trust or have complete faith, which is needed to be able to create.*** We need to understand that to the degree we trust and believe that we are an aware creator, to that degree we will be able to manifest.

We will now discuss Jesus' mystery or hidden teaching about sowing word-thought seeds and what happens to it. The biblical Mark is really one of the best and most precise summaries of manifesting anywhere available. Notably, 1 Cor 2:7 reads, "We speak about the mystery of God's wisdom. It is a wisdom that has been hidden, which God had planned for our glory before the world began."

MARK 4:1-32 (NKJ): Self-mastery - How our feelings create our life

And he began again to teach by the seaside: and there was gathered unto him a great multitude, so that he entered into a ship, and sat in the sea; and the whole multitude was by the sea on the land. ² And he taught them many things by **parables**, and said unto them **in his doctrine,** ³ Hearken; Behold, there went out a sower to sow: ⁴ and it came to pass, as he sowed, some fell by the way side, and the fowls of the air came and devoured it up. ⁵ And some fell on stony ground, where it had not much earth; and immediately it sprang up, because it had no depth of earth: ⁶ but when the sun was up, it was scorched; and because it had no root, it withered away. ⁷ And some fell among thorns, and the thorns grew up, and choked it, and it yielded no fruit. ⁸ And other fell on good ground and did yield fruit that sprang up and increased; and brought forth, some thirty, and some sixty, and some a hundred. ⁹ And he said unto them, **He that hath ears to hear, let him hear.** ¹⁰ And when he was alone, they that were about him with the twelve asked of him the parable. ¹¹ And he said unto them, Unto you it is given to know **the mystery of the kingdom of God: but unto them that are without, all these things are done in parables: ¹² that seeing they may see, and not perceive; and hearing they may hear, and not understand;** lest at any time they should be converted, and *their* sins should have forgiven them. ¹³ **And he said unto them, know ye not this parable? And how then will ye know all parables?**

Verse 1
Jesus here is talking to a multitude of people. **Remember Jesus was saying in Luke 12:31, "But rather seek ye the kingdom and all these things will be added onto you."** He is also confirming there is abundance available for everyone in the kingdom.

We really do need to understand this kingdom or realm and its way of doing things first before we can really live in endless abundance.

Verse 2
A doctrine or dogma is a truth or the mind of somebody.

Philippians 2:5 says, "Let this mind be in you which was also in Christ Jesus." We all need to understand the mind of Christ, and this was called his teaching. **We also know that he had many followers due this teaching of his.**

Verse 3-8
Jesus talks about a farmer sowing agricultural seed which is the first part of the parable. This is Jesus' best-known teaching. He talks of four different situations in which the Sower places his seed. One brings forth thirty -fold, one sixty-fold and one even hundred-fold. Three of this produce none or little harvest.

Jesus agrees with Genesis 8:22, "As long as the earth endures, seed time and harvest ... shall not cease."

Verse 9
Here Jesus is telling his followers to really hear what he is saying. He wants his listeners not to hear but to understand (comprehend) what he is saying. John 8:32 says, "And you shall know (understand) the truth, and the truth (your understanding) shall set you free." Again, to live in abundance, it is crucial to completely understand this fundamental knowledge or technique for manifestation.

Verse 10-12
Jesus is now only talking to his disciples. The disciples realised that there is more to this parable than just agricultural information and that there was hidden spiritual information in what he was saying. He suggests that there is a ***spiritual principle***, a strategy, a technique, we need to understand to experience total happiness and abundance on earth. Here Jesus is telling his disciples that there is a mystery or hidden teaching about the Kingdom of "God."

The Kingdom of "God" is not a place or event where you need to go or are going. It is all one unseen creative and powerful energy field or realm within and among everybody to rule and control this kingdom (this quantum energy field) we now live in.

In Luke 17:20-21, ***Jesus said that this kingdom does not come with signs to be observed or visible display but is within and among you.*** If the residents of any kingdom understand the way things in that kingdom work, they will be able to and are allowed to use the creative power of that kingdom or realm.

This most powerful force and technology to be used, as already proven now, is within us. This kingdom and its powerful creative energy reside in us and is for everybody on earth to be used and this was the good news about the kingdom Paul was bringing to the gentiles (non-Jews).

We are all holy and divine, and sons (descendants) of this heavenly kingdom and have the authority to use its powerful creative energy. He was also saying that it will be those who understand this parable who will be able and will have the skill to bring forth abundance in their life. Mathew 6:32-33 says, **"But seek ye first the Kingdom of God and his righteousness and all these things shall be added unto you."** So, we need to, and it is essential that we first seek, find, and understand this kingdom and its ways of doing things before permanent abundance will show up in our life. We do now know that we are all just magnets for miracles and can deliberately choose to have abundance in our life.

[13] And He said to them, **"Do you not understand this parable? How then will you understand all the parables**? [14] The sower **sows the word**. [15] And these are the ones by the wayside where the word is sown. When they hear, Satan comes immediately and takes away the word that was **sown in their hearts.** [16] These likewise are the ones sown on stony ground who, then they hear the word, immediately receive it with gladness; [17] and they have no root in themselves, and so endure only for a time. Afterward, when tribulation or persecution arises for the word's sake, immediately they stumble. [18] Now these are the ones sown among thorns; they are the ones who hear the word, [19] and the cares of this world, the deceitfulness of riches, and the desires for other things entering in choke the word, and it becomes unfruitful. [20] But these are the ones sown on good ground, those who hear the word, accept it, and bear fruit: some thirtyfold, some sixty, and some a hundred."

Verse 13

Jesus said that this is a key to all other parables. If we understand this parable or story, we will also understand all his other parables or stories. All parables are parallels meaning whatever is true in the natural will be confirmed in the spiritual. *Here Jesus is giving us a truth in the natural, then following it up by the same truth in the spiritual.* Here he also emphasises the importance of understanding how this kingdom we are already living in is working.

John 3:3 states, "...except a man be born again he cannot see the Kingdom of God," meaning that we need to exit the realm of natural thinking to be able to enter the realm of supernatural thinking. We need to stop our usual way of understanding and open our spiritual eyes and ears.

Verse 14
Jesus is repeating the parable but makes a meaningful change. He no longer talks about an agricultural seed but a word seed. An idea or thought (word) is a spiritual seed that operates on the same laws as an agricultural seed. The word seed responds precisely the same way the agricultural seed does. Here Jesus is explaining how to use the creative power of thought (word) and emotion in our life. The physical (seen) world comes out of the non-physical (unseen) world, and we have the language to speak to it with our feelings to change things in our life. This means **the feelings that happens inside our bodies has a direct effect on the stuff our world is made of.**

Important to know that this word-seed was sown into the body's heart. Our feelings in our body's hearts change our life in and around us. Our life will be according to our true feelings in our heart. For a thought to be sewn into our heart, a heartfelt emotion needed to be attached to it forming a feeling seed. Whatever we choose to experience in our life cannot be from the ego-mind, but we must first have a good feeling in our heart about it. A thought or affirmation from your ego-mind without an emotion has no creative power at all. A thought is just a realisation of an idea with no creative power to create on its own.

As discussed before there are eight basic emotions in life which are anger, fear, sadness, disgust, surprise, anticipation, trust, and joy, of which trust (love) and fear (distrust) are the two most essential energies at the core of the human emotional experience. Fear is the most significant emotional killer of all of our dreams and desires, where trust is the surest emotional way of fulfilling them.

FEELINGS AND EMOTIONS, THE BIG DIFFERENCE
The divine intelligence created emotions and feelings to help us to rule and be in control of our own lives and our own reality. A feeling is not an emotion. There is a significant difference between the two, and we need to be aware of the differences to be able to create correctly.

A fundamental difference between emotions and feelings is that **feelings are experienced consciously,** it is a choice, while **emotions can be experienced subconsciously or consciously.**
a) Emotion is a <u>bodily reaction</u> activated through neurotransmitters and hormones released by the brain. (With emotion, chemicals are released in your body as a consequence of an interpretation of a specific trigger, and you get a feeling when you think about it in your mind). **Emotions then are just the end product** or a record of past experiences.
b) Feelings are the <u>conscious chosen experience</u> of an emotional reaction.

A feeling is a conscious mental picture of what is going on in your body when you have an emotion. It is generated in the heart and related to one's higher truth and it is true hundred present of time. **Emotions are physical in nature** and can be seen and measured, whereas feelings are very subtle, difficult to understand and cannot be measured.

Just remember that all experiences always have an emotion attached to it.

How you feel is how in-tune you are with how reality really is. You do not have a choice about your emotions, meaning that there are no wrong emotions. If you do want to change them, you need to change your thoughts about the experience that is causing them.

Also, essential to know is that the body does not know the difference between an experience that causes an emotion or an emotion that you can fabricate by thought alone. Your emotions and feelings are not a guide for what you should do. If you want to change your emotion on any subject, you just need to change your thoughts and focus on them.

A thought is just an idea, and where your thoughts and attention are going, is where your emotions (energy, power) and then feelings will flow. If you want something, give it your undivided attention and if you do not want something, look elsewhere by changing your thoughts and attention about it to something more positive. The easiest way is to become aware that you are aware, and the negative thought will disappear. You need to always think about what you think about. You need to connect your thoughts and attention to the future and disconnect them from the past. When you change a thought and the attention of the thought, you are causing the feeling of the thought to change, which will then change your destiny.

Feelings are something you choose from the inner depths of your being and are never wrong because that is how you truly feel. You will unavoidably always experience your genuine feelings. If you choose to change your feelings, which you can do at any time, you can change your destiny. Remember that you can have whatever emotion you are having (e.g., crying, anger), but you are never to allow yourself to forget who you genuinely are. You need to realise who and what you are and that everything is a manifestation of this divine energy field.

Meditation will help you to work on your response to different situations and overcome your emotions. Once accomplished, your mind can only respond to the feelings in your heart.

Verse 16 – 20

There is an electromagnetic field of energy in and around us, and we speak to this energy field with our feelings which is a combination of our thoughts and emotions. Thoughts (words) are seeds of e.g., goodness, truth, beauty, abundance, etc, that you plant in the garden or energy field of your mind. When you have a thought (a word, an intention) and an emotion on anything, you have given it life, forming a feeling seed, now planted, and getting cultivated in the garden of your heart. From the heart it emits energy and then becomes your reality.

We now know that any thought of anybody that has an emotion added or attached to it will form a thought-feeling seed that will grow by drawing the same energy frequency from the field. You are planting ***thought-feeling seeds*** when you have thoughts with an added emotion on anything. You deposit the thought-feelings seeds in your subconscious mind. So, in the end your thoughts will become things. You need to ensure that you add the appropriate emotion to any thought you want to grow.

When planted into the field of our heart, a word-seed or thought-***feeling seed*** (thought plus emotion) will also grow according to how we keep our focus and intent.

If we put our ***feelings*** and focus (attention) into anything it will grow and as said before this principle is for everybody. If the Sower plants a thought-***feeling*** seed into a ***heart*** that is like the wayside, the ***focus*** and therefore the manifestation will immediately disappear. When he sows a thought-***feeling*** seed into a stony heart, losing his ***focus***, no root system will develop, meaning the manifestation will not grow for too long. When he plants a thought-***feeling*** seed in a weed-infested heart where double-mindedness rules, he slowly loses his ***focus*** and vision, eventually causing them to lose their manifestation. Luke 8:7 says, "...and the thorns sprang up with it (the thought-***feeling*** seed) and choked it."

When we sow a thought-***feeling*** seed into good ground the harvest will manifest and increase manifold.

As in the natural way, the thought-feeling seed will grow quickly and supernaturally, and the desired manifestation will happen without any effort from our side.

You are going to reap the ***exact fruits*** according to the seeds you are sowing in your heart. You can have anything you desire. What you imagine and expect will come to you. Whatever you sow is what you will reap, so you need long and short-term desires. Every thought you think with the slightest emotion is causing a feeling, and as long as you maintain this new modified state of your body, they will become things, creating your future.

You also need to know exactly what you want and what you are sowing and cultivating in your heart and broadcasting, emitting into the electromagnetic field so that you can recognise your harvest when it comes. If you sow a corn seed, you will only reap corn, and if you sow an apple seed, you will only reap apples. Corn seed in the ground ***emits and draws exactly the same vibrational frequency energy from the universal energy field as itself,*** which then manifest into a stalk of corn. *It is the field then that creates the matter, and not the matter that creates matter.*

You need to know precisely what kind of seed you are being, seeing that that is what you will radiate, attract, and manifest. You, as a type of seed, will also emit and draw the same energy frequency from the energy field as the template of your state of being you created of yourself. This means you must be and act like the person you want to be and want to experience. Manifesting then is adjusting your own vibrational frequency to who you really are and what you want to experience.

Again, you need to connect your thoughts and emotions to the future and disconnect them from the past, otherwise you will harvest precisely the same stuff as in the past.

You need to have a clear desire and always keep your *focus*. (A general desire has a less clear desire and less focus.) Remember, the outside world is a holographic mirror of your thoughts and emotions in your mind. Always also expect the best harvest, and you need to never chase after any creative proses, it will always come to you.

If you change your idea of who you are, your personality changes, and you emit a different message into the universe which will then manifest accordingly.

We can use this electromagnetic energy system as a technology or method to manifest our own peaceful, joyful, and loving world.

So, a feeling consisting of a thought and emotion in the heart creates an electric and magnetic wave which is the language the field recognises to manifest. This changes the electromagnetic field inside the atoms in our body, around us and radiates (emits) the electromagnetic waves possibly indefinitely into the quantum energy field (field of possibilities) where your desires are drawn from. This has been proven over the last 20 years without doubt by Dr Bruce Lipton with *epigenetics,* which says you can change your body by thought alone and demonstrated it scientifically with the placebo and nocebo effect. *Neuroplasticity* has now also proved that you could change your brain by thought alone.

Our traditional idea of prayer, where we are pleading, begging, and crying for our needs out of a position of lack or of not enough, e.g., appealing for rain, for peace, or for health, will never be successful because it is mixed with doubt. If you desire anything, it always needs to be attached to an expectation, a trust, an allowing, and an absence of any resistant thought that it will happen.

Doubt is causing ninety-nine per cent of our desires not to realise. If you pray to ask for anything you acknowledge, imply, or affirm, it does not exist, and it will not happen. We have seen that a feeling of doubt (distrust) also manifests power and what you doubt (e.g., I cannot, I do not, I cannot have) you will still, create or manifest due to this creative power. Chasing after any needs is also just doubt in action. You need to choose your thoughts and desires not out of a position that you are not good enough but out of a position of worthiness, trust, gratitude, and a feeling as if it is already being answered. You need to change your habits of how you think and feel. Feel the feeling as if the prayer is already answered. You are already blessed and not will be blessed.

The energy field does not recognise your voice but your state of being (your mood or feeling) that you create in your heart. The feeling in your heart then is your state of being and is the prayer language that speaks to the energy field and forces of creation around you, who then reacts. This then means that there is nobody you can pray to, to ask for anything seeing that you are in control of your own destiny. You simply need to stop your wrong thinking and choose to create everything for yourself.

You are always in the receptive mode of something you feel. Whatever feeling seed you sow, good or bad, is precisely what you will reap, and you also cannot hide from it. Always listen and find alignment in your feelings before you ever react or create anything. You must have a satisfying thought and non-resistant feeling for your ideal creation. **Do not fake it, what you feel, is what you feel.** The heart emanates (radiates) the electromagnetic waves of our desires and attracts, draws like a magnet out of the field of possibilities our desired manifestation.

Feelings are the seed and yes, we are the sowers and therefore the powerful creators of our own destiny.

²¹ And He was saying to them, "A lamp is not brought to be put under a [a]basket, is it, or under a bed? Is it not *brought* to be put on the lampstand? ²² For nothing is hidden, except to be revealed; nor has *anything* been secret, but that it would come to light. ²³ ***If anyone has ears to hear, let him hear.*** " ²⁴ And He was saying to them, "Take care what you listen to. [b]***By your standard of measure it will be measured to you; and more will be given you besides.*** ²⁵ ***For whoever has, to him more shall be given; and whoever does not have, even what he has shall be taken away from him.*** ²⁶ And He was saying, "**The kingdom of God** is like a man who casts seed upon the soil; ²⁷ and he goes to bed at night and gets up by day, and the seed sprouts and grows—how, he himself does not know. ²⁸ The soil produces crops by itself, first the blade, then the head, then the mature grain in the head. ²⁹ But when the crop permits, he immediately [c]puts in the sickle, because the harvest has come."³⁰ And He said, "How shall we [d] picture the **kingdom of God**, or by what parable shall we present it? ³¹ *It is* like a mustard seed, which, when sown upon the soil, though it is smaller than all the seeds that are upon the soil, ³² yet when it is sown, it grows up and becomes larger than all the garden plants and forms large branches; so that THE BIRDS OF THE [e]AIR can NEST UNDER ITS SHADE."³³ With many such parables He was speaking the word to them, so far as they were able to hear it; ³⁴ and He did not speak to them without a parable; but He was explaining everything privately to His own disciples.

Verse 22

If you have any feelings, they will start to grow and manifest whether you want them to grow or not. Every thought-feeling seed will manifest, good or bad. Any emotional thought will grow. Nothing will be hidden, it will grow. Thoughts and emotions will become things in your life. In Acts 10:34 Peter says, "God shows no partiality and is no respecter of persons." It grows for everybody, good or bad, whether we know this kingdom's power (energy field) exists or not. The quantum energy field always says yes to any thought-feeling seed.

Again, feelings are the secret to creating life. We can now exactly create the desired life we want to live.

Verse 23-25

Jesus said that we just need to understand. We need to understand (comprehend) this revelation and trust this technique or formula, saying that those that have ears to hear must listen carefully so that they can understand. Jesus is explaining to his disciples that to the degree they understand this truth to that degree will they trust and receive of what they desire. The more we understand (comprehend) this method, truth, or technique the more we can trust that our specific desires and feelings will always manifest.

A large part of agriculture is weeding, meaning we need to eliminate wrong unwanted thoughts. Matthew 13:19 states, "While anyone hears the word of the kingdom and does not grasp and comprehend it, the evil one comes and snatches away what was sown in his heart."

To be able to have an abundant life, it is essentially important that one understands this teaching correctly. Again, we are only abundant as we can let ourselves be. Proverbs 4:23 says, "Above all else, guard your heart for everything you do flows from it." What you think and feel is what you plant in your heart. The heart is the source from where you will experience your whole life.

What is in your heart is the thought-feelings seed that you will manifest. You also need to hold steadfast and guard your feelings seed for the manifestation of your desires.

In Mark 11:23 Jesus again says, "and does not doubt in his heart but believes that those things which he says will be done, he will have whatever he says." Hebrews 11:1 also states, "Now faith is the substance of things hope for, the evidence of things not seen" Again, we need to **protect our hearts** from negative self-talk and also negative talk to others, e.g. gossiping, shaming, critiquing, inappropriate jokes, judging people, blaming, lying, comparing, violent news, and movies, or anything that influences our emotions negatively and lowers our vibration and then the attraction from the universe. We will lose ourselves (our aware self) and be back in our ego-mind again, where we will be unable to create. If we do expose our mind to negative talk and negative information, we produce within us a low vibration that prevents us from our own well-being and wanted creation.

We need to **walk in truth** so that the discipline of our actions comes from the heart and not out of obligation.

We are creating our own destiny, and we need never to doubt that we are creators busy creating our own life.

In the beginning of this book, I mentioned that there are no accidents and that we create our own reality, and that includes you reading this book at this moment in time. There are only thoughts and feelings, and the universe always says yes to all the feelings we are radiating. Therefore you and you alone have drawn these teachings into your experience at this moment in your life.

Verse 26-29
We cannot control the process. There is no need for us to help in the growth process. Jesus explains that we do not need to understand how the thought-feeling seeds will grow and manifest in our hearts. The process of growth is automatic, supernatural, and effortless. We now have a better idea how it works scientifically but surely still do not fully understand it. We have seen that feelings in the heart create an electromagnetic wave that radiates into the energy field (field of possibilities). Scientists agree, saying it emits into eternity and therefore will never disappear.

The quantum energy field (Kingdom of God, the god force) causes the feeling-seed to grow and manifest. While you cannot see it, the solution is already here. The only part we need to play is to stand firm (keep our focus and attention constant) in knowing who we are and maintain our focus and intent on the desired thought. With our feelings as a guiding system of what is wanted, we also need to trust that all our desires will come to pass.

Verse 30-32
Jesus again compares the kingdom's power to the power of a mustard seed. "God" has given the same power to this kingdom that he has

given to an agricultural mustard seed. Again, our thought is the image of the quantum energy possibility, and if you add an emotion, it forms a seed that you plant in the field of your heart where the field cause it to grow.

Our heart is the field where the thought-feeling seeds from our minds are planted and cultivated.

Irrespective of what thought it might be, if it is coupled with emotion inside an already fertile heart the thought will respond the same way the mustard seed does when a farmer sows it into good ground. What we hold in our heart, meaning our feelings, becomes the truth of our world. Interestingly we also see that, that explained how the biblical "God" created in Genesis. This technique or method to create is exactly the same for us to use according to our current scientific knowledge. We see that reality was not created through action but through thought energy. The universe was not an accident. "God" spoke it into existence with specificity and clarity, creating from the unseen to the seen. Please have a look and see in Genesis 1:3-26 where "God" created the world, "God" first said the word seed (unseen), then he saw (seen) it, and even said at the end that it was all good, meaning he had a positive emotional feeling about it.

We also read in Hebrews 11:3, "we know that the world and the stars, in fact all things were …made at God's command (word seed); and that they were all made from things that cannot be seen (from the unseen)."

Waiting for things to happen to you then is wrong. You now need to choose and create your own life by sowing thought-feeling seeds. This concept that makes reality manifest does also not need action as we used to understand. (Action creates a powerful change in our trust or belief and thus helps in the creating proses.)

In the end, there is no other existence except the one we live in. There is no end to it at all. At this moment, we are in heaven. We are already living in eternity; this life and moment are all there is. This is a never-ending world.

As divine human beings, we are constantly expanding, so we will always have desires and will never come to a position where we will be able to say we have enough. This world is our world, and it is our co-creation. We are kings in this kingdom. A king of any kingdom has all the power he needs to create the life he wants, and so do we.

We create the life we want to live in this kingdom by the thoughts and emotions we choose to have. We do not need to ask or pray but only decide what we want. There is no earthly power anywhere that can compete against us, and there is nothing we cannot be, do, or have. You can also see that there is no such thing as luck, you create your own luck. Life will be as good to you as you are letting it be.

THE GOSPEL OF THOMAS AND FEELINGS

The Gospel of Thomas (discovered in 1945) is undoubtedly one of the earliest accounts of the teachings and sayings of Jesus. It claims to contain revelations and parables only made known to the apostle Judas Thomas (Didymus, the twin). It also is regarded by some as the *single most important find in understanding early Christianity outside the New Testament.*

Here Jesus is explaining the kingdom and how to use your <u>feelings as a language to speak to this energy field</u>.

The Gospel of Thomas, in saying 113;

His disciples said to him. "When will the kingdom come?" **Jesus** said, "It will not come by waiting for it. It will not be a matter of saying 'Here it is' or 'There it is.' Rather, the **kingdom of the father is spread out upon the earth and people do not see it.**" Jesus here proclaims that the power of the Kingdom of "God" is already present on earth and, as we now know was always present on earth, and people just could not see or understand it. The power is within and working equally for Jesus, and everybody on earth but can only be controlled by those who see (hear, comprehend) and understand this secret hidden message of Jesus.

The Gospel of Thomas, in saying 3;
Jesus said, "If those who lead you say to you, 'See the kingdom is in the sky,' then the birds of the sky will precede you. If they say to you, 'It is in the sea,' then the fish will precede you. **Rather, the kingdom is inside you, and it is outside you.** When you know yourself, then you will be known, and you will know that you are a child of the Living Father; but **if you do not know yourself, you will live in vain and you will be vanity (useless, empty)."**

Here again, we can see that the kingdom of God is not a place or event that will happen in future but an internal state within and around us. In the second part, Jesus re-affirms that we need to know our true nature otherwise, we will live an unsuccessful life. We really need to know that we are powerful, sacred, holy, and divine.

The Gospel of Thomas, in saying 70;
Jesus said, **"If you bring forth what is within you, what you bring forth will save you."** If you do not bring forth what is within you, what you do not bring forth will destroy you." In his actual words, Jesus also explains that within us is all the possibilities and that we need to bring them forth to salvage our own lives. Salvation (saved from harm, danger, or loss) which is offered to everybody, is not on our outside, it is within, and it is for now and into eternity.

We have the ability within to think ourselves better and be saved, but we must choose to execute the decision to bring forth what is within us.

The Gospel of Thomas, in saying 48;
Jesus said, '**If two make peace with each other in this one house,** they will say to the mountain, 'Move away,' and it will move away." **Your house (your human feelings) is** a unity of your brain (mind, thoughts) and your body (where you experience chemical bodily emotions). As long as the brain (mind, thoughts) and the body (emotions) are double-minded or in opposition to each other, there is doubt, and no unity and no manifestation can happen. When your brain (mind, thoughts) and your body (emotions) are in unity and full of trust in your house (your whole human being), forming or causing a feeling in

the heart, you become a powerful creator, and mountains can indeed be moved. Jesus says that if you can organise and align your mind (thoughts) and body (emotions) in one direction with a feeling and keep the focus, everything you desire will be created.

The electromagnetic field does not recognise your words (voice) as a prayer request but only the feelings you are radiating as a prayer request. Thoughts are the language of the brain (mind) and emotions the language of the body, and feelings in the heart are the language of the house (your whole human being) as one unit that the energy field understands and reacts to, causing the desired experience. This was exactly what Jesus wanted to share with us.

How you feel is the current state you are in as a human being and is the life you are living and, therefore, also your destiny. Just like an apple or corn seed, to manifest, you need to be one whole human unit in your thinking and feeling. If you trust it, it will be realised. It has been said "As a man thinks in his heart, so is he." We do now know you can change that anytime you desire to. If you are sensitive to how you feel, you will know precisely what you are doing with your thoughts and then your future life.

The Gospel of Thomas, in saying 106;

Jesus said, "When you make the two one, you will become the sons of man, and when you say, 'Mountain, move away,' it will move away."

Here again, we see that when your thoughts (your mind) and your emotions (your body) agree and are one in your feelings (your human house), you will be as powerful as Jesus. Here we see that Jesus suggests that you need to have unity in your thoughts and emotions to become a powerful creator. Your true feelings are what you are in unity with and the language the universe will react to. When you have unity of any desire, you can trust and not doubt that the specific desire will manifest.

You need to have no hidden motives and be surrounded by your answer with a feeling of trust and gratitude. ***You cannot have a desire for and against the same thing.*** This means you need always to ask what you truly feel in your heart, without the ego-mind interfering. Remember to assume the feeling that would be yours as if you already possessed your wish. Again, we see that salvation (recovery) comes through proper understanding and trusting of this knowledge (teachings) of Jesus Christ, rather than through faith in him as a person or god as we understood it in the past. The power of the kingdom upon the earth is within and around us, and there is no other known earthly power that can compete against us.

It always manifests all possibilities for everybody who has got unity and no doubt in their thoughts (mind) and emotions (body) about anything. Everybody means every human being on earth irrespective of who they are or what they have done.

The truth is that our true essence or deep identity is inside us, and it is this powerful kingdom in us that Jesus was talking about in Luke 17:20-21, even saying *the kingdom does not come with signs to be observed or with a visible display but is within you and among you.* In 1 Cor 4:20, we read, *"For the kingdom of God is not in word but in power."* You really have true creative power, whether you believe it or not. Jesus' whole teaching in Mark 4 confirms that our old understanding that "God" is a personal and interventional "God" and is responsible for the things that happen to us is not acceptable anymore and is simply wrong. The kingdom in us will empower, inform, and guide us on how to make happen what we desire to make happen. We just need to listen to our true, higher, eternal selves. Do not ever make this kingdom's reality imperfect.

WORTHINESS:
We do need to feel worthy to have a self-confident abundant feeling which is needed to manifest and receive any of our desires. The universe only gives us what we think we are worthy to receive, and *if we know our true divine identity, we will always feel that we are worthy.* Any but any unworthiness blocks any positive desired manifestation. If you think you are unworthy, you will never, but never receive your desires, but instead what you do not want.

You need to long for the genuine truth and need to open your own gift, and if you really want the truth, you will question what I am questioning and then your own truth will set you free. In John 8:31-32 we read, to the Jews who had believed him, Jesus said, "*If you hold to my teaching, you are really disciples (followers of him).* Then you will know the truth, and the truth will set you free."

In John 3:3 we read, "Except a man be born again, he cannot see the kingdom," meaning we need to change our way of thinking to be able to see, understand and thus, as he said, be born into this kingdom again and understand then its ways of thinking and operating.

Jesus' knowledge, truths and his vision are his only gift to you. Be dependent on yourself, your thoughts, and your ideas about life. Be your own saviour, trust your own greatness and do not trust your outside for your freedom and happiness. Feelings never lie, what you feel is precisely what you will manifest, so decide and listen to your feelings while you manifest your desires. *How you feel is your indication of how you are in harmony with your inner being.* Always be aware of what you are feeling and thinking about. Your feelings are your state of being, and your state of being creates your destiny. The universe wishes to bring everybody happiness, peace, freedom, joy, and abundance, are you able to receive it?

If you feel abundant and worthy, you will generate wealth.

The universe is waiting for us to request from it all our desires, saying that *when you ask, it is being given.* We can now manifest our own peaceful, joyful, and loving world. We are more than the limits we have imposed on ourselves; we are capable and worthy. Change the way you look at things, and the things you look at (your destiny) will change and then everything will be a miracle. You now need to take responsibility for your own life and change it to your desired life. There are no accidents or specific miracles in life, only thoughts, feelings, and emotions. Remember, "Dragons live with the people who feed them."

We are not to spend time fighting dragons projected by the mind but must learn to observe them while being detached from them. *There is a divine intelligence within you to guide you. If you do not like your life, repent (change your way of thinking), train your mind, and choose new thoughts.* Your new thoughts will take you there and you can tell whether it is good by how you feel. All things are possible, never resist any good thought with a negative contradictory thought. If you release your resistance to any desired thought, your desire will become more prominent and real.

You will also realise that you always must live a sincere life of honesty and integrity. Whatever you need will come into your experience if you are pure and authentic. *If you do not live an honest, sincere, and authentic life, your thinking will be distorted, and you will create accordingly.* It will cause insecurity and doubt because you will feel you are not worthy receiving your desires.

We do not need divine help, we are divine, we choose our thoughts, and we change them. Our cultured way of outsourcing our own well-being and survival to another person e.g., Jesus, is not an efficient and acceptable way to live by anymore. We manifest our own salvation (deliverance) in this world through our individual and collective thoughts and feelings in line with how we want to experience our life. We cannot ask somebody else to pay, sacrifice or intervene (being a go-between) for our own wrong thinking which the bible call sins because only we alone are able to control and change our wrong thoughts (sins), which will lead to our salvation (recovery) and happiness in our life, right now here on earth.

As we can see, we also cannot worship any messenger of this truth that was defined by many mystics including Jesus at the time. *We can see that it is about the message and not the messenger.* We are all one, no one person or individual identity can ever be worshipped.

Our traditional idea of "God" controlling and causing our world to happen is just not acceptable anymore. I do not want to use the word "God" because by using this word, you are talking about a personality which is an image, object or quantity that makes this energy field small with a humanlike character created by man, which cannot be accurate. Our traditional image of "God" as a being with an identity and an authoritarian and patriarchal personality and an imagined friend are human cultural inventions and do not exist. As you can see, there is or cannot be any personal God, somebody whom we are separate from and who is interfering personally in our everyday activities. The source of consciousness ("God" within) can understandably also have no form or image at all. Using godly at least is a quality or condition, so instead use godly, which explains quality as a non-personality.

Godly is a non-dualistic, non-separate energy inside and around us, and we are all part of this one energy.

"God", as we understood it in the past, was an image (object) where godly is an energy, a state, a condition or quality of pure consciousness, awareness and beingness. Religion does not exist because that would mean separation or dualism is part of oneness and that just is not even scientific possible and therefore cannot exist.

Because of our memories from the past of unexplained suffering, "God" as an image separate from us and in control of everything can often bring feelings of insecurity, causing doubt with again no creative ability. God as we understand it in the past is just an invention by humans, creating a god in humans own image. Seeing also that this energy field pervades all things, if we worship anybody, we actually are worshipping this one energy field that incorporates every one of us.

As we now also realise and as we used to think in the past, the universe will never ever test us.

YOUR SUBCONSCIOUS MIND AND FEELINGS

For an exceptionally long time, we ignored our subconscious mind, and we cannot do it anymore. **Your subconscious mind which is like a hard disc on a computer runs your life and is your connection between your mind and the universal conscious mind (energy field). The subconscious mind is the most crucial factor in your ability to manifest what you desire.**

Your subconscious mind is permanently in contact with the universal conscious intelligence (quantum energy field). **Your real self-image or self-identity (your ego or false sense of self) of whom you think you are, functions from this software program in your subconscious mind.** Your life is an expression of your subconscious thoughts and shaping your reality. Everything your subconscious mind (habitual mind) thinks and believes will come true, it rules your life, and you can change it any time you want.

Your subconscious mind then has been programmed or conditioned with past feeling experiences and uses that to create your new experience on anything you are focusing a thought and feeling on. The universe, quantum energy field, only reacts to your subconscious mind. If you **focus on anything and trust** that it will happen, it will be created precisely as a programmed or conditioned past experience in your subconscious mind. This then means **you are only as strong as your subconscious thinking.**

Your subconscious thoughts shape your reality from past experiences. **Every thought-feeling makes a subconscious impression.** Fortunately, only the true thought-feelings in your subconscious mind have the power to create and manifest, whether good or bad. This means that the only way to have abundance in your life is by reprogramming your subconscious mind to habitually think and believe that it is in your life right now.

More than ninety per cent of your approximately six to twelve thousand daily thoughts come not from your conscious but from your subconscious mind. Your conscious mind is as strong as your subconscious mind, but the subconscious mind works most of the time while your conscious mind is only switched on for ten presents of the time. If you then want to change anything, you will need to change the habitual thought-feelings programmed or conditioned in your subconscious mind.

Our subconscious mind as a hardwired disc is just a storage system like a computer, it is there to safeguard, and protect us from creating stuff in our conscious mind that can harm us e.g., wants, hopes, and needs that is not part of who we really are. Our future life will primary reflect the most emotionally charged recurrent images we picture of ourselves on the screen of our subconscious mind. The subconscious mind also consists of environmental and genetic input.

This then means we need to be continuously through our daily activities be conscious of our subconscious mind which also puts thoughts in our mind that we do not want anymore, and therefore needs to be controlled by us with our conscious mind by us being aware of this principle. The only subconscious thoughts that can influence us are the thoughts that we make active with an added feeling, otherwise they are totally powerless. Your mind is playing games with you, and you need to learn how to stop it and take control of your own life. If you do not like the thought in your conscious mind, just change your attention away to a more positive thought. All things are possible, but you only attract things in alignment with the thought-feeling you are experiencing (your vibrational frequency).

Our conscious mind is the creative mind, but it is not effective in creating anything if it does not agree with our programmed subconscious mind. (The energy field will not allow you to interact or attract anything that you do not have access to in your subconscious mind.) As we now know, *if we want to change or reprogram our subconscious mind and our self-image, we need to replace it with our true divine identity of who we really are.*

Our subconscious mind cannot distinguish between what is real and what is imagined, and only responds to whatever is put into it. Our subconscious mind does not know the difference between witnessing, imagining, or living an experience. Our subconscious mind does not know the difference between positive and negative emotions but only the level of the emotions.

We as human beings manifest unconsciously continuously with our feelings (the unity of our thoughts and emotions). To impress the subconscious with the desirable state, you need to assume the feeling that would be yours had you already realised your wish. The quantum energy field reacts and always says yes to every true feeling and will manifest accordingly. *Always look for the best feeling thoughts you can find.*

As mentioned before, the energy field (universal source) is reacting to anything we give an emotion to, which we can choose to change deliberately at any time to change our destiny. This helps us to fulfil all our dreams and desires. If you can see it in your mind, you can feel it in your hand, so what pictures are you holding on to the screen of your mind to shape and fulfil your life?

Your thoughts and real emotions (love/trust to fear/doubt) have creative power, and the degree of the creative power depends on the degree of the power of your feelings. At the centre of your being, you are still a creator with creative power, so even if your feelings are not what you need or desire, you will still manifest every one of them.

Fear (doubt) inactivates a good thought and helps a negative thought activate and manifested. Fear (doubt) is the opposite of love and trust, meaning it will help any negative thought to be still fearfully created.

So, it is vitally important to know that only what you feel, and trust subconsciously will happen and manifest in your experience. Do not ever leave any room for "I wonder if." Any feeling of doubt, lack, insecurity, and comparison all stand in the way of you attracting your specific desire. Again, if it feels good, give it your full attention, and if it feels bad, withdraw your attention to something else.

The subconscious mind accepts feelings as its language. ***To change the subconscious mind to what you want to experience is to reprogram your habitual feelings (habitual thoughts and emotions) in your subconscious mind.***

The only way to have what you desire in your life is that your subconscious mind must be reprogrammed through thoughts that are accompanied by the right feeling experience until it becomes a habit.

There are basically three ways to reprogram your subconscious mind permanently, which are the following:
a) Repetitive thoughts e.g., affirmations with emotion, can move a thought from the conscious to the subconscious. (This is by far the most important way to change your subconscious mind forming new brain circuits.)
b) Autohypnosis while in a theta state when your subconscious mind is open just before sleep.
c) Super-learning energy psychology e.g., Psych K.

You need to always be in a receiving mode for all your desired manifestations. To manifest correctly is difficult if what you want is in opposition to what you experience, but that does not need to prevent you from changing your thinking and emotions. **You cannot have a desire for and against the same thing.** Your wishes, wants, needs, and hopes that something will happen cannot and will not ever manifest because wants, needs, buts, and hopes are a lack of trust (doubt), resulting in no power or low vibration and then resulting in no manifestation. **You cannot have a lack of trust, a may be, a hope, a doubt or a want and still receive.** Doubt (lack of trust) will cause manifestations of what you do not want. Trust causes a constant vibration which you need for manifestation. You cannot hope for something to happen, and you need to trust it will happen. Be ready in your mind that it is on its way and trust that you will receive it, and it will be done.

If you do not know the power of your thoughts, you will end up thinking very dangerous thoughts. Do not allow your thoughts to go to anything you do not want. **Do not ever complain on your journey concerning your manifestation because that will surely stop or slow it.** Remember always, "where focus goes, power flows." The power in us can do harm or good. Ultimately, life is neither suffering nor perfect happiness. It is what you trust it would be, and the choice is always yours. Negative unwanted thoughts like the idea that something terrible will happen, focusing on lack or saying I cannot, bring misfortune and has precisely the same creative power but in the opposite direction. Fake it until you make it is wrong and won't manifest because you need to change your state of being and not just your thoughts. The universe is also not here to punish you but can only respond to the vibrational frequency pattern radiating by you and your feelings.

The universe responds to you and gives you more of whatever you feel whether good or bad. You have control over what is, so you become the magnet of your own destiny. Make peace with what is, take the path of no resistance and advance confidently in the direction of your dreams. You must have a strong vibration to fulfil your specific desire and not something that stands in the way like a wrong contradictory resistant thought. The frequency of your vibration needs to line up with the frequency of your desire with no contradictory thoughts.

Only you are in control of your own vibrational frequency, and therefore only you attract your own experiences in life. Sinful thoughts (wrong and resistant contradictory thoughts) will always punish you because of the creative energy field that manifests all good thoughts, and also all wrong, unwanted thoughts. Therefore, Jesus tells us not to sin, meaning having wrong unwanted contradictory thoughts. The path in your mind that has got no resistance is the right path. Repent again, means you need to change your way of thinking. If you change your thinking, the rest of your life will fall in place. Remember, although all things are possible, always live an authentic and honest life.

All your thought feelings, including your unwanted, sinful thoughts, will come back to you as real experiences. You will get what you think about whether you want it or not.

The only cause of human suffering is oneself. We must always choose the right thoughts we are radiating into the universe. We create our own suffering and create our own hell with the unwanted thoughts and emotions we are radiating because we are not controlling them. This was Buddha's main conclusion also. What you call fate is just a life situation you have created for yourself subconsciously. We are never allowed to abandon our attention to our thought processes, especially in the face of any threat to our safety. We need to take our attention away from our problems and from unwanted thoughts and things. Always look for the next logical step. Do not ever talk against your own desires or about what is missing from them. Sometimes the only thing that keeps us from moving to where we want to go is talking too much about where we are at the moment. We need to learn to live in our wholeness every day and are never allowed to dwell on our imperfections or on things that we are not. Again, the universe only gives us what we honestly think and feel we are worthy of and expect to receive.

Each of us will manifest in alignment with our personality, which includes our ego (our false idea of self) in our subconscious mind. We just need to stop having wrong unwanted thoughts. This means that we need to stop sinning (having wrong thinking) because we will get punished by sin (wrong thinking) and not for our sin (wrong resistant thoughts). **If we struggle or suffer, it is because of our thinking in our subconscious mind that is wrong, and not the universe that has something against us**. As mentioned before the universe will never test us. We must make peace with what is because even the slightest fear or doubt will create accordingly. What we trust in our subconscious mind will always happen, so we need to listen to our emotional guidance system, and our feelings to see whether our thinking is correct. We need to be in control of our own thoughts and eliminate any contradictory thinking deliberately and quickly, which is always possible. Always reach for the best feeling thought you can find that has no resistants. The same thoughts as in the past will always lead to the same results in the future.

You need to live in the feeling of being the one you want to be. The fastest and best way to reprogram our subconscious mind and then our state of being is to come to the true knowledge of our own true divine identity. We need to do things because that is who we really are. It also depends on how much we know and trust that we genuinely are eternal divine creators. Remember that more than ninety per cent of the way we live our daily life comes from our subconscious minds. If you know who you are, then change your feelings accordingly, you are changing your subconscious mind which then change your personality and destiny.

If you know and trust the truth of who you really are, you will erase your past identity and personality and become a brand-new person. You will heal your past by the true knowledge of who you really are as consciousness.

If you know who you are, the love that you think you get from the outside e.g., material possessions, power or relationships, is unnecessary because of all the love you experienced yourself on the inside. What is also beautiful is that the more whole you feel, all the things and experiences you wanted in the past, you no longer yearn for.

Happiness, kindness, tolerance, self-control, love, peace, and goodness is also not a product of what you achieve, do, or get, and it is a quality of what and who you already are.

As in the traditional eastern way, there is no reason for this knowledge to take years to come into your reality. This revelation knowledge can really come into maturity overnight by you fully understand this knowledge. Repent and change your mind about the way you are thinking of yourself and the way you did things in the past.

Again, Jesus' only gift to you was his revelations and his knowledge, his good news that you now also can know, understand, trust, and then walk in the same powerful way as he did. As Jesus, know your feelings intimately and learn to trust and have faith in them, and let whatever process or experience just happen. You can be enlightened and walk in the same or even more creative power as Jesus did. He said so and literally meant just that. In John 14:12 Jesus said, "Most assuredly I say to you, he who believes in me, the works that I do he will also do; and **greater works than these he will do** because I go to My Father." As mentioned before, Jesus realised, and we need to realise the truth that we are all divine and filled with this creative power, and miracles will also be drawn and follow us, as it happened with Jesus. <u>We must always remember that manifesting at the centre is really designed to increase our self-awareness of our true identity.</u> *We are already infinite, powerful, and eternal. We always need to be aware that we are awareness that is aware and will forever be aware.*

As stated, the purpose of life is to know our true identity and to be used by the universal consciousness in order that the universal consciousness may experience and enjoy itself in all its aspects. Through experiences in life, we also return back to our original self-knowing. We are here for the experience and to enjoy life, nobody has authority over us. Remember, only who we are and not any manifestation will finally satisfy us. This is not a technique or formula to fix our exterior world but to fix our interior world. *Our circumstances do not even matter, only our state of being matters.* (Remember that how we think and how we feel creates our state of being.)

For the first time ever, everybody in this world can all live a peaceful, happy, wonderful, and luxurious life.

You can change everything. You are only limited by the lack of your imagination and the lack of you keeping your attention (focus) on the pictures you hold in your mind. You only suffer at the hand of your own imagination. If you can dream it, you can have it, so what do you desire? Changing your inner world and your outer world will change, and what you need will come to you. Again, you attract what you are and not what you want. Everything you want already exist outside this dimension and is already busy coming to you, you just need to, and you can decide how long it will take to arrive.

There is nowhere else, no other existence except here, this one you are living in now. You came here to enjoy and experience your life in the here and in the now, and whenever you change your energy vibration, you change your life. There is no way home. This is it; you are not on a journey to any destination somewhere else. This is home, paradise, heaven, and life. This now will go on forever into eternity. Renewal (salvation) of your life is for now and not for one day in the future. All possibilities and probabilities already exist in the form of energy right now. The only way to discover your desires is to communicate to this limitless energy field using your feelings.

You do indeed finally write your own story. What you feel determines your life thus, the only thing that matters is how you feel. When your body and mind die here on earth, the real you will still be here to experience life in whatever form is desirable for you as this energy field. Whatever you can see in your imagination and feel in your heart, you can hold in your hand. Everything is here in energy form, and it is yours already. You will see it when you first can feel it. Only do desire things that feel good, and you are sure of and expect to become real for you. You need to decide to do a thought experiment to confirm all these truths. The more you manifest, the more you will realise that you are divine and can trust it, and so it will become part of your usual way of living.

I want to end this chapter by stating again that the manifestations only help you recognise and then transform you closer to your

authentic true self. Who the real you are, your true origin will become clearer for you which will cause you to be more joyful, peaceful and happy. When you know your true nature, most desires and fears lose their meaning. You will also realise that when you feel whole, you have fewer needs and desires to live your everyday life. If there are no desires, all things are at peace. It is not what you do or have; it is that you know that you indeed are an eternal divine being.

You will only truly be happy if you manifest your desires from knowing your true identity. You are worthy to enter heaven now; heaven is really just disguising itself. Life will not happen elsewhere in the future but here and now. There is no other time but now. This now is eternity, and it has got nothing to do with time; this is the infinite appearing finite. This is paradise, and this is home. The fact is you and heaven are the same thing. Eternity has no place or time. This now has no moment in time; it never starts and never stops.

You indeed are a miracle of life. You are not whom you see in the mirror, you are the source of all phenomena, a vibrational creator, the attractor of all your experiences in life, and feelings are the language to attract it all. There is no ending to what and who you really are. Only you know your own truth. Completely trust yourself; your true higher eternal self has the power to attract any desired possibility. So, keep your ideas and desires to yourself because others can put doubt in your creative process, which will lead your inability to manifest your specific desire.

The satisfaction for life is not coming later. You are not on a path, you are at home; in fact, you never left. You are coming and going is nowhere but where you are. You are already and always were in eternity (heaven), and you can and need to design and regulate your own life here and now from all these creative possibilities. The world will be a mirror or reflection of what you think in your mind and feel in your heart, so you need to choose to feel happy and divine knowingly. Jesus even said, *"Those who have more, more will be given,"* and he meant just that. Do not set yourself any limitations, you are unlimited, infinite and worthy.

Everything is continuously unfolding and is becoming for you. ***You are on a never-ending expanding journey. You did not just come for the outcome of your story, but also for the experience and happiness it brings.*** Everything is always working out for your best. Surrender, yield to the flow of life. Whatever the present moment contains, accept it as if you had chosen it, work with it and not against it, and then you change it. Always be ready because you are forever on the brink of experiencing all the things that you desire.

This is it; this present now moment is all there is. This is and always has been everyone's eternal home. We are eternal, timeless energy beings, and there is nothing better or ever will be better than being alive right here at home and right now. Wherever we are, it will be here and now.

We did descent from heaven as consciousness and therefore we're before our birth and will be here after our death. When we as a human die, we leave our form (body) and past (mind) behind while our consciousness still goes on. Birth and death do not restrict us. After death, we will be what we were before our birth, namely consciousness.

When we die, we will not be locked up in a dark room doing and experiencing nothing. Our true identity as consciousness/awareness cannot have an experience of nothing but can only continually expand by choosing a new experience to enjoy in whatever dimension and aspect of itself it prefers.

The world cannot satisfy you. We as an earthly personality really only want to manifest something for the emotional happy response we will get from it, because we think it will make us feel happy, but this fragmented happiness will not last. Happiness is an eternal part and always with us as part of our true identity. Anything we do on behalf of the body for the body is impermanent and will disappear one day, and only our true aware identity will be left.

Keep in mind that the ultimate basis of happiness and satisfaction is to recognize yourself as pure consciousness.

We must live out the richness and fullness of who we are and whom we are meant to be.

You are no longer a prisoner of your past and can now deliberately go to the destination of your own choosing. You and the intelligence that created this infinite universe are the same spirit within. **We genuinely are divine beings with divine power, and with any clear intention and elevated emotion,** there is no limitation in what we can manifest; all things are really possible.

You will never see something in your mind that you cannot manifest. How do you want to live the rest of your life? *You need now to actively start to live as if you do accept your actual identity and you do realise the power that is accompanying it; otherwise, this knowledge will also be just mind knowledge.*

CHAPTER 4

STILLNESS MEDITATION: WHY AND HOW TO CONNECT TO OUR HIGHER ETERNAL TRUE SELF

We as god in physical form that made this universe, has detached and lost our connection to consciousness and need to regain it. Consciousness is the field of pure awareness. There is a place deep inside us that is absolutely pure, a place where we can be the whole quantum energy field. A place deep down where we are just the fabric and structure of existence itself, a place nobody is allowed to invade. A place where we are not somebody but being our higher or true self as this quantum energy field. A place where there is no separate self but only our higher aware being, which is the real us. A place where we non-define ourselves, where we are nobody and just being aware. *That is why being aware of being aware is the highest form of meditation.*

Time is one of the most valuable gifts we can and need to give ourselves. We need time to put our old beliefs aside for a moment and have a look at meditation, which is now scientifically being proven to be genuinely effective and the *single most powerful spiritual practice there is.*

Our beingness and the experiencing of it are totally mixed, and we can separate the two with meditation. Our being should not be governed by our minds. *Our mind is the source of all our joy and suffering* and stillness meditation is a vehicle that will lead and direct us to our higher self and then to ultimate happiness. Our mind is just a memory or bundle of past and future thoughts. Every awaken moment of the day we are focused on something. We have been conditioned our whole life to focus only on objects including our thoughts, emotions, perceptions, things, and circumstances, but we need to be aware of the source of all this attention. We need to learn not to follow what the mind thinks and tells us what he wants us to do but learn to follow our true feelings from our higher aware inner self only. We need to connect to the whole of who we are, our higher inner self.

Meditation is the most effective tool for us to be who we really are and also to observe the mind objectively. Meditation means to become familiar with. There is no objective except to be entirely in the here and now. Meditation is not for improving us but for learning to become completely present, thoughtless, conscious, and aware of who we really are in this eternal here and now moment. With stillness meditation, we stop talking and thinking and become aware and familiar with our true higher inner being within us. With true meditation all thoughts stop, and all resistance stops, which allows our vibration to rise and synchronise with our pure non-resistant energy vibration. When we are thinking, we are not in the present moment but in the past or the future and are running a program from the subconscious mind.

1) Stillness meditation as a thoughtless state
All spiritual teachings point us to being one with that which we are. When all activity ceases, and we are simply aware of just being, we are meditating. *A state where we are not concentrating on any image and no thoughts arise, where we are thoughtless and in the now, is called meditation.* True meditation is to stop thinking temporarily,

and without any thoughts, there is no mind; there will then be neither the sight nor the seer. We are simply witnesses or an observer of our own thought processes, not part of it or becoming involved with it. We are aware of the thought but just rest as awareness. We do go within and become aware of who we are as awareness itself and be aware of who is being aware. It also helps us to gain self-control. Thinking is just talking to ourselves, whereas here we do not use our minds and are in a ***thoughtless state.***

Stillness meditation is when we are not bodily or mentally doing anything at all, and are in an empty, thoughtless state of mind where no thought arises, which also means there are no resistant thoughts. Meditation has no specific purpose but is about understanding ourselves and being who we are as awareness itself. **We do not meditate on anything, we just meditate, just being aware.** We are not concentrating on anything; all activity ceases, and we are just in a state of ***beingness.***

With meditation we come to feel our basic inseparability from the whole universe. The easier we can connect to the unseen energy field (your eternal inner being), the surer we will feel that there is a power greater than us that is working full-time through our thoughts and emotions. If we allow ourselves to stop thinking and just be, we will find that we are in the eternal here and now. We need to understand it rather than just practice it.

We do not do meditation as an activity but being in a state of awareness or beingness of who we really are. We are pure awareness, being or observing only. We rest in our true nature before any thought arises where we are formless and timeless. With meditation, we are being aware or observing without reacting, judging, or giving an opinion on our thoughts. It is an ability to distance and separate ourselves from our finite thoughts and emotions. We then will start sensing space which means we are not thinking anymore. We keep our attention in neutral, away from any image in our past or future (we are in the timeless now). We focus on nothing and remove all our thoughts and sensations of our body from this reality. ***You need to become nobody, nothing, no time, no place, and then you become***

infinite awareness. The quantum energy field exists beyond our thoughts and sensations. This can only be experienced in the now by our pure awareness. When we are in the now moment, we are in a meditative state. Our vibrational frequency also do tend to raise because if we stop our thoughts, we also stop our resistant thoughts causing our energy vibration to rise. We are simply being and sitting silently and witnessing, observing the thoughts that are passing before us from a neutral place. We are not judging them or interfering with them. We need to be conscious of them without allowing our minds to try to control or to become attached to them; we observe from a neutral place.

If we judge, getting involved with our thoughts, we lose the pure awareness or pure observing of it, and we are in the thinking process, which is our mind again. The idea is to create a gap between awareness (the observer) and our mind. We are not a doer but a watcher of our thoughts. If you are giving attention to a thought, you are thinking and not just meditating. We are in a thoughtless state and totally disengaged from all that arises, and our mind is resting in who we really are as consciousness. With true meditation, we are just pure awareness, and our body is experiencing death in life. We cannot do or practice it but only understand it. As you can also see, there is no place for visualisation or imagination in this thoughtless state of meditation.

2) Stillness creative meditation with non-resistant thoughts

You can and will never stop desiring, and as we have seen, every answer you need to every desire is literally inside you right now. In the space where you are only awareness, there is a silence wiser than any guru, book, seminar etc. Deep within, we have a direct line to the unseen conscious field. Your mind does not need the ego-mind to control it but needs to be controlled by your consciousness. There is a vast realm of intelligence beyond thought. Here you ask your higher inner self or the energy field what it wants for you in each of your specific life experiences and focus your mind on the details of what you want. You can never stop thinking (offering a vibration) but can deliberately control your own thoughts (your vibrational offering). **You decide what thoughts you want to have, and you surrender by listening to the answer rather than making the answer happen.**

Your higher inner self (energy field) is aware of everything and knows exactly what you need and are looking for. Your higher inner self also knows the path of least resistance. In your higher inner self, there is clarity and a solution that exists already for every problem in your life. Clarity is the internal quest to find the vibrational equivalency of your higher inner self. With feelings, you have your own guidance system. Your higher inner self (the quantum energy field) follows your thinking and will always give you the best answer with your best feeling for the answer. Nobody can give you better advice or direction than your own higher inner self. You need to take care of yourself and find your own answers in the eternal now; nobody else can do it for you. No other person can talk to your higher inner self on your behalf.

No saint, guru or pastor can be your mediator and advice you on the next step towards your desire. The quieter you can become, the better you will be able to connect and hear from your higher inner self for the path of each desire you need to follow. Meditation with concentration is a way for your inner being to teach you alignment.

In meditation with concentration, you reach into your higher inner self and when you are in alignment you can trust the message you get from it to make your own decisions. A quieted mind and focus on nothing but space slow down your brainwaves to a theta state which puts you in a more receptive mode.

With stillness and through your thoughts (concentrating), you will also be able to tune in and hear the energy field (inner self) in the now (eternity) communicating to you through vibrational frequencies (feelings) giving you guidance in the direction you need to go. Your inner self is having a thought at the moment you have a thought about any subject, and the way you feel is your indication of how in harmony your thoughts are with your inner self. Your brain is a frequency analyser, so you only know certain things, but you expand your frequency bandwidth through meditation. You need to know what your higher inner self knows and vibrates. You then need to become a vibrational equivalent of your higher inner self. The path in your mind that has no resistance, follow that. You need to tune out the clutter of your resistant thoughts in order to hear the fine, clear vibration. You need to focus on wanted thoughts only, ignoring unwanted thoughts.

Consciousness or the quantum energy field cannot communicate or talk to you with words, but through vibrational frequencies (feelings). A feeling is a conscious awareness of a vibrational frequency. You need to choose the correct vibrations and feeling and then translate it into words, impulses, emotions, sensing, inner knowing (you know that you know), or gut feeling and react accordingly. The more you are in this kind of receiving mode, the more intuitions, impulses, etc., you will receive to lead you. You then react and manifest according to the strength of your realisation. The more you trust, rely on, and become familiar with your feelings and your higher inner self, the more you will be assured and want to trust yourself.

You are always in a receptive mode, and your feelings are the power to live life the best way possible; listen to them.

The energy field is informative and wants to and will reply to any guidance you will need. Remember that you cannot know everything in your mind and thoughts that arise are also not always yours. All the information is inside us, so we certainly do not need advice from anybody else. **You need to realign with your higher inner self for all your answers and live from there.** Your higher inner self is the best person and supreme teacher to go to for the path to the fulfilment of all your desires. 1 John 2:27 again says, "But the anointing (this powerful energy) which you have received from Him abides in you and you do not need that anyone teach you, but as the same anointing teaches you concerning all things, and is true, and is not a lie, and just as it has taught you, you will abide in Him." Consciousness (this energy field) is not in your brain, but your brain is a receiver tapped into this information in consciousness (in this energy field). You know all truth and just need to follow your own guidance system, meaning your feelings.

The brain or mind is only a record of our environment and our past and only helps us to stay the same to survive. Our inner self will always lead us to the whole we want to be. If our mind is still and peaceful in the now, ideas will flow a lot easier to us. Nothing changes before we do not change our thoughts, emotions, and feelings about it. If we want to change, we need to get new knowledge that is available only in this eternal now moment from our higher self. Our higher inner self knows what stands in our way of receiving. So, we need to stop, sit still, and quiet our mind (our lower self) so that our higher inner self can speak to us in the now, informing us what to do.

The mind can never be in the present eternal now moment where all new knowledge and possibilities exist. If we only use our mind, instead of being in the now, we will always concentrate on some image in the past or the future that does not exist. Concentrating alone cannot ever be in the now. The mind is just a record or residue of the past and only works in the past or future and cannot be in the eternal now. The problem then is that all our immediate decisions are decided by our subconscious mind with its programmed memories from the past.

To get different experiences in future, we need then to get guidance in the now moment and not from the past. ***Only in the present moment do we have access to other possibilities.*** This now moment is always new and alive and is always an unfolding mystery, so it is always better to enquire from our higher inner self that is timeless and is always in the now with all the answers of the universe.

We cannot go along the whole day according to what we in our mind think we want to do because only feelings and not thinking thoughts are in the now, and that is what we need to follow. When we are enquiring from our own inner true being for guidance, it will be in the now and be reflected in our mind.

We need to make sure our desires stem from our higher self and our wholeness and not from our lower ego-self.

Our pure desires are what the energy field seeks to express through us and will also give us the best feeling. To get to a place where our desires are pure, our thoughts and feelings must be in alignment with our desires. Through stillness, we can realise which thoughts and emotions cause our pure feelings and pure desires.

Remember, all thought feelings are creative, good, or bad.

Stillness meditation with concentration will help to stop or slow our thoughts so that we do not have any resistant thoughts. We need to get in a state of non-resistant thoughts, having a non-resistant mind. Contradictory thoughts or resistant thoughts will prevent any desired manifestation. Do not talk yourself into resistance. When we quiet our minds, the higher self will not have any resistance. The absence of any resistant thought will cause an allowance of our desire. We also always need to have sincere, truthful thoughts.

When we come into the now moment, there are no emotions, and we are left with only feelings. We need to listen and honour our pure and best feelings, which are our compass to show us direction. We need to be in agreement and in alignment with everything we desire. If we get a negative thought, we need to just replace it with a more positive thought. Always take the path of non-resistance. There is always a better feeling choice.

Imagination is the greatest creative faculty we possess.

Forming a clear visual template (through visualization or imagination) of what it feels like to have the answer in our thought process can help us to be more positive. We need to hold the picture in our hearts and live by it. There is no limit to what we can do. A clear vision or intention in any direction with a feeling will accordingly manifest it for us.

If our thoughts and feelings align of our higher inner self (the energy field) and we respond accordingly, our desires will indeed be fulfilled.

Although the energy field will answer us in many different ways, it will always answer us. We must also to follow and listen to our higher aware self when it gives us direction through intuitive ideas, impulses, dreams, signs etc. As mentioned before, all possibilities we desire already exist in the unseen energy field in the timeless now. To live the ultimate life, we need to align our whole life with the present now moment.

What we really feel and not what we think will happen for us. With our mind, we lock in the desired possibilities, and with our heart (feelings), we give the possibilities life. (We need to desire with our feelings what we want to make a reality to us).

Feelings are really life's secret power to abundance, so you must take care of them. The world around you will be a mirror of the feelings you harbour within. You are constantly emitting information into the universe, and your biggest decision is for you to decide whether you want to live in an unfriendly or friendly universe. You can now create your own new life. Your external world can change amazingly fast, and it is easier than ever before if you change your inner world. You do not wait for experiences from the outside for your feelings to change anymore, you can now deliberately control your feelings from the inside, so that you can be your own deliberate creator.

The universe only reacts to your feeling vibration and not to your words or thoughts. You do not need any luck; you can now call all those things which do not exist as if they do. You can now select a new possibility in the quantum field and begin to emotionally embrace that future for the appropriate vibration, and your desire will manifest. You can and need to test the universe to see whether this rediscovered knowledge is accurate and trustworthy.

How you feel is what matters most. What you feel is the best for you will be the best for everybody else also. You always need to do what you genuinely feel like and always live in the direction of all your dreams. You really need to feel your way and live from one experience to the next. Nothing is worth it if it does not make you feel happy.

This is the best time to be alive. Before this earth's foundation you consciously decided to come here at this moment in time to enjoy and experience life itself. You live here on earth now, you moved in. The world you are live in is changing rapidly, and you need to wake up and start to follow your heart and its feelings and thereby control your own life. You can be, have and are connected to everything you want. Trust in the wholeness of who you are, and do not give up your power for anything.

You are the only feeler of your feelings. Always only follow and live according to your true feelings and your own experiences, and you can never be wrong. Rest in who you are, your true divine identity, then your living will be authentic, and you will experience genuine happiness from within and also absolute freedom right here and right now. Transform your life from habit into a choice, compulsion into consciousness and move from unawareness to awareness. Stay in the flow and only do that what you honestly feel makes you happy.

There is no more, and this is all you need to know. ***The entire universe is backing you up and waiting for your instructions.*** Without limitations, you can have everything you desire. You are totally free, and the only thing that is keeping you back is your thoughts about yourself and the way how you imagine you want to live your life on earth. You need to figure this all out, and the universe will help you to create your future by sending you the next logical step. All your desires will make their way toward you. You do know way more than you think you do. You need to trust yourself and your instincts a lot more.

Life is a journey, not a destination. Anything you can dream up in this life can be achieved; prepare yourself for receiving! Are your desires big enough to be worthy of you?

May something you could never dream of before now happen to you!

CHAPTER 5

CONCLUSION

You as the holy and divine decided to come here. You have placed yourself on this earth from the unseen energy field to the seen at this present moment in time and space to manifest and display what only you will be able to display. *The fact then that you are in this world, which is by your choice, makes you incredibly special, needed, and important.* You are also unique and exactly whom you needed to be, and nothing would have been the same if you did not exist. So, you can be authentic in all you do.

We have awakened ourselves now. We have learned that we are not divided and are one with the essence of this divine quantum energy field and are here to express and expand this energy field or consciousness. We have realised that we are the unseen energy field manifesting ourselves to whatever we desire, and in our case, it is in the human flesh. *We cannot go back from whom we now are.* We are all one with everything, and everything is one. We are everything and everything is in consciousness. So, we have discovered who we are and that we are here for the joy of being here. We all have unique paths and are here to give our unique gifts to the world. We have learnt that we are in a union and not divided from the universal energy field. *We are not even human but need to be alive so that the universe can experience itself through us.*

There really is only one powerful energy kingdom or realm on earth, and its ways are the only way how manifesting happens here on earth. It is for everybody who wants to know how it works. The universe will always say yes to any feeling that you are radiating out into the magnetic field. We have learned that we need to change our way of thinking before we can change our circumstances. We are creating our own life with every thought and emotion, so we need always to be aware of our own thoughts.

We can be whomever we desire to be, and we can experience whatever we desire to experience. We use this available creative energy freely to experience life on earth. How we use this energy is how we experience life. We need to do our own thinking and imagination, and nobody else can do it for us. We have learnt that the energy field is speaking and guiding us is through our feelings. A quieted mind will put us in the optimum receptive mode.

We have realised that when we discover who we really are, heaven opens for us here and now. We can also trust the truth that there is no shortage or lack of anything here. Our feelings are our prayers that will manifest into our reality, not our thoughts or our words. We also need to listen to our feelings which will direct us like a compass in the direction we should go. *We set the rules so we cannot blame anybody if our harvest is different from our desires.* Even our genes and, therefore our bodies and health depend on the quality of our thoughts. If we change our perception, we can even change our own genes.

A beautiful way somebody once said it was that a man who lives in meditation would never die. Although we discussed stillness meditation, meditation is not separate from life. Living continuously and consciously in a spirit of alertness, awareness, and mindfulness is the most important part of meditation; *listen to your impulses.*

The most meaningful kind of freedom is knowing and never forgetting who and what you are. See that life is beautiful, and the world is a better world with you in it. Freedom is not a fantastic place but a knowing of who you actually are.

There is no end here, only a place where you leave this story. When you are finished, you will just drop your mind and body (earth suit). You then become hundred percent divine energy again. Remember you are part of infinity and a unique, whole, powerful, free, and a beautiful being. You came here to experience life. The whole part of you is all "God." Knowing that you are whole and complete, the things that you love will also always follow you. Although we are all just stardust rapped in skin, just an appearance in consciousness, there is no higher power than us.

Stay aware, and do not risk your awareness for anything. Listen to your own intuition, listen, and take care of your own thoughts, trust your feelings, and follow your heart and everything is possible; you cannot fail. Wherever you go, only follow your feelings, not your thoughts. The universe wants to expand its own expression through you and show you who you really are. You can now manifest all your wildest desires, make sure how you feel; the better you feel, the better it goes.

Be your authentic self, and your life will be full of goodness, magic, passion, and miracles, and will always work out for you. There really is only one of us here, so just love oneness and then do whatever you feel like doing. ***You are holy, sacred, and divine, peace, joy and love will always follow you, and yes, the best is still to come.***

A few notable proverbs:

Anna Brown said, "Welcome home to the home you never left."

Rupert Spira quoted, "I searched for myself and found only God, and *I searched for God and only found myself."*

Rumi said, "It is your road and yours alone. Others may walk it with you, but no one can walk it for you." Me, "I was searching for God my whole life until I realised it was me, I was searching for, now I am happy."

Sadguru said, "Most people do not even know who they really are, but they have opinions about everything and everybody else. Are you allowing their opinions to dictate the nature of your existence?"

APPENDIX

Mooji, a spiritual teacher said, "The one who is open, receives. The one who is hungry, eats. The one who doubts, delays. The one who sees is free." He also said, "The one who knows the self, is the self."

If you never realise you are awareness experiencing life through a vessel, you will continue to identify yourself as a body and mind and one day will die and just return back into the unified quantum field. Just remember that the laws of physics have ruled out immortality.

The greatest gift we can give our children is to allow them to be who they really are. Their true divine nature free them, and let them, and allow them to go in the direction that they feel to go instead of us dictating them to go.

Nikola Tesla, an electrical engineer said, "Peace in the world can only come as a natural consequence of universal enlightenment." If people wake up and know who they really are, they will not behave the way they do anymore.

THANK YOU:

Greg Braden (Author, new age)
Prof. Brian Cox (Physicist)
Prof. Sean Carroll (Physicist)
Jesus Christ (Christian bible)
Richard Dawkins (Biologist)
Past. Creflo Dollar (Christianity)
Ahmed Hoosen Deedat (Islam)
Dr. Wayne Dyer (Author)
Dr. Joe Dispenza (Neuroscientist)
Albert Einstein (Physicist)
Eckhard Tolle (Spiritual teacher)
Prof. Bart Ehrman (Historian)
Rabbi T. Friedman (Judaism)
Esther Hicks (Author)
Nassim Haramein (Physicist)
Sam Harris (Neuroscientist)
Christopher Hitchens (Author)
Dr. Michio Kaku (Physicist)
Prof. Lawrence Krause (Physicist)
Deepak Chopra (Physician)
Dr. Robert L. Kuhn (Author)
Dr. Bruce Lipton (Biologist)

Sri Nasargadatta Maharaj, Ramana Maharshi (Hindu sages)
Aaron Abke (Spiritual teacher)
Mike Dooley (Author)
Mooji (Spiritual teacher)
Past. Joel Osteen (Christianity)
Prof. Elaine Pagels (Gnostic Gospels)
Paul (Christian bible)
Sri H.W.L. Poonja-Papaji (Indian sage)
Shadguru (Indian yogi)
Sri Rajneesh, Osho (Mystic)
Rabbi Tovia Singer (Judaism)
Rupert Spira (Spiritual teacher)
Sunny Sharma (Meditator)
Thomas (Dead sea scrolls)
Nikola Tesla (Elect. Engineer)
Neil deGrasse Tyson (Scientist)
Prof. David Tong (Physicist)
Neale Donald Walsh (Author)
Alan Watts (Zen Bhuddism)

www.ingramcontent.com/pod-product-compliance
Lightning Source LLC
Chambersburg PA
CBHW050235120526
44590CB00016B/2097